Edited by
Zvi Bodie,
Laurence B. Siegel, and
Rodney N. Sullivan, CFA

The Future of Life-Cycle Saving and Investing: The Retirement Phase

RESEARCH FOUNDATION

OF CFA INSTITUTE

Statement of Purpose

The Research Foundation of CFA Institute is a not-for-profit organization established to promote the development and dissemination of relevant research for investment practitioners worldwide.

ISBN 978-1-934667-26-2

5 October 2009

Editorial Staff

Maryann Dupes
Book Editor

Cathy Gentry
Assistant Editor

Cindy Maisannes
Publishing Technology Specialist

Lois Carrier
Production Specialist

Biographies

Lans Bovenberg is scientific director of the research network Netspar (Network for Studies on Pensions, Aging and Retirement), in which various pension funds, insurance companies, public agencies, and universities participate. The second Dutch social scientist to win the Spinoza Prize, Dr. Bovenberg used the prize money to found Netspar. Previously, he was a professor of economics at Tilburg University, where he served as scientific director of the Center for Economic Research. Prior to that, he was deputy director of CPB Netherlands Bureau for Economic Policy Analysis (Centraal Planbureau). He worked at the Dutch Ministry of Economic Affairs in the Hague after starting his career as an economist at the International Monetary Fund. Lans Bovenberg has published extensively in leading international journals on public economics, tax policy, environmental economics, institutional economics, pensions and aging, international macroeconomics, and labor economics. He holds a PhD from the University of California, Berkeley.

Peter Diamond is an Institute Professor and professor of economics at Massachusetts Institute of Technology. Professor Diamond has served as president of the American Economic Association, president of the Econometric Society, and president of the National Academy of Social Insurance. He is a fellow of the American Academy of Arts and Sciences and a member of the National Academy of Sciences. Professor Diamond has written on behavioral economics, public finance, social insurance, uncertainty and search theories, and macroeconomics. He has served as a consultant on social security reform to the U.S. Congress and the World Bank and has written about social security in Chile, China, France, Germany, Italy, the Netherlands, Spain, Sweden, the United Kingdom, and the United States. Professor Diamond was chair of the Panel on Privatization of Social Security of the National Academy of Social Insurance. His recent books include *Taxation, Incomplete Markets and Social Security*, *Social Security Reform*, and *Saving Social Security: A Balanced Approach* (with Peter R. Orszag), and *Reforming Pensions: Principles and Policy Choices* (with Nicholas Barr), with a shortened version, *Pension Reform: A Short Guide*, upcoming. Professor Diamond holds a BA in mathematics, summa cum laude, from Yale University and a PhD in economics from MIT.

Amy Finkelstein is a professor of economics at the Massachusetts Institute of Technology. Professor Finkelstein is also the co-director of the Public Economics Program at the National Bureau of Economic Research, where she is a research associate, and is co-editor of the *Journal of Public Economics*. Previously, she was a junior fellow at the Harvard Society of Fellows. Professor Finkelstein has received numerous awards and fellowships, including a Sloan Research Fellowship, the 2008 Elaine Bennett research prize, and the 2008 TIAA-CREF Paul

A. Samuelson Award for outstanding scholarly writing on issues related to lifelong financial security. Her research on public finance and health economics focuses on market failures and government intervention in insurance markets as well as the impact of public policy on the health care sector. Professor Finkelstein received an AB in government, summa cum laude, from Harvard University and an MPhil in economics from Oxford University, where she was a Marshall Scholar. She holds a PhD in economics from MIT.

David Laibson is a Harvard College Professor and the Robert I. Goldman Professor of Economics at Harvard University. He is also a member of the National Bureau of Economic Research and serves on numerous editorial boards as well as the boards of the Health and Retirement Survey and the Pension Research Council. Professor Laibson is a recipient of a Marshall Scholarship and of grants from the National Science Foundation, the MacArthur Foundation, the National Institute on Aging, the Sloan Foundation, the U.S. Social Security Administration, and the Financial Industry Regulatory Authority. He has received the Phi Beta Kappa Prize for Excellence in Teaching and is frequently cited in such leading publications as the *New York Times*, *Wall Street Journal*, and *Financial Times* as well as the PBS program *Wealthtrack* and the Bloomberg television network. Professor Laibson holds a BA in economics, summa cum laude, from Harvard University, an MSc in econometrics and mathematical economics from the London School of Economics and Political Science, and a PhD in economics from Massachusetts Institute of Technology.

Robert C. Merton is the John and Natty McArthur University Professor at the Harvard Business School. Professor Merton is currently the developer of SmartNest, a pension management system that addresses deficiencies associated with traditional defined-benefit and defined-contribution plans. Previously, he was a senior adviser to Salomon Inc. and JPMorgan and a co-founder and principal of Long-Term Capital Management. Prior to that, Professor Merton served on the MIT Sloan School of Management finance faculty. He is past president of the American Finance Association, a member of the National Academy of Sciences, and a fellow of the American Academy of Arts and Sciences. Professor Merton received the inaugural Financial Engineer of the Year Award from the International Association of Financial Engineers as well as the Alfred Nobel Memorial Prize in Economic Sciences (with Myron Scholes) for a new method to price derivative securities. He holds a BS in engineering mathematics from Columbia University, an MS in applied mathematics from California Institute of Technology, a PhD in economics from Massachusetts Institute of Technology, and honorary degrees from the University of Chicago, Claremont Graduate University, and seven foreign universities.

Alicia H. Munnell is the Peter F. Drucker Professor of Management Sciences at Boston College's Carroll School of Management and also the director of the Center for Retirement Research at Boston College. Previously, Professor Munnell was a member of the President's Council of Economic Advisers and Assistant Secretary of the Treasury for Economic Policy. Prior to that, she served as senior vice president and director of research at the Federal Reserve Bank of Boston. Professor Munnell has published many articles, authored numerous books, and edited several volumes on tax policy, U.S. Social Security, public and private pensions, and productivity. She was co-founder and first president of the National Academy of Social Insurance and is currently a member of the American Academy of Arts and Sciences, the Institute of Medicine, and the Pension Research Council at the Wharton School, University of Pennsylvania. Professor Munnell is a member of the board of the Century Foundation, the National Bureau of Economic Research, and the Pension Rights Center. She was awarded the International INA Prize for Insurance Sciences by the Accademia Nazionale dei Lincei in Rome. Professor Munnell holds a BA from Wellesley College, an MA from Boston University, and a PhD from Harvard University.

Anna Rappaport is president and founder of Anna Rappaport Consulting. Previously, she worked for Mercer Human Resource Consulting. Ms. Rappaport chairs the Society of Actuaries Committee on Post-Retirement Needs and Risks and has been a leader in the development of an extensive set of research on the post-retirement period. Currently a fellow, she has served as president of the Society of Actuaries. Ms. Rappaport serves on the boards of the Women's Institute for a Secure Retirement and the Pension Research Council. She is a member of the Chicago Network, an organization of the top women in Chicago from all walks of life. Appointed a senior fellow on pensions and retirement by The Conference Board, Ms. Rappaport provides input to the organization and its mature workforce initiative on pensions and retirement issues. She holds a master's of business administration from the University of Chicago.

Paul A. Samuelson is Institute Professor Emeritus at the Massachusetts Institute of Technology. Professor Samuelson received the Nobel Prize in Economics. He serves on the Finance Committee of the National Academy of Sciences. He was an economic adviser to Presidents Kennedy and Johnson and has been a consultant to the U.S. Federal Reserve, U.S. Treasury, and the Congressional Budget Office. Professor Samuelson was an early contributor to the new modern theory of finance and long served as a trustee of TIAA–CREF. Aside from having authored a best-selling introductory economics textbook, *Economics*, translated into more than 40 languages, he wrote *Foundations of Economic Analysis*. Five volumes of *The Collected Scientific Papers of Paul A. Samuelson* have appeared, and sixth and seventh volumes are in preparation. With Robert Solow and other joint authors, he has contributed to several dozen books on economic theory and policy. Professor Samuelson holds a BA from Chicago University and an MA and PhD from Harvard University.

Jonathan Skinner is the John Sloan Dickey Third Century Professor of Economics and a professor with the Dartmouth Institute for Health Policy and Clinical Practice and Family and Community Medicine at Dartmouth Medical School. Before moving to Dartmouth, Professor Skinner taught at the University of Virginia. He is also a research associate with the National Bureau of Economic Research in Cambridge, Massachusetts, and a former editor of the *Journal of Human Resources*. A recipient of a Robert Wood Johnson Foundation Investigator Award in 2006–2008, Professor Skinner was elected to the Institute of Medicine of the National Academy of Sciences in 2007. His research interests include the economics of government transfer programs, technology growth and disparities in health care, and savings behavior of aging Baby Boomers.

Robert M. Solow is Institute Professor Emeritus at the Massachusetts Institute of Technology, where he is a professor of economics. Professor Solow is currently Foundation Scholar at the Russell Sage Foundation. Previously, he taught macroeconomics and other subjects to undergraduate and graduate students. Professor Solow has served as a member and chairman of the Board of Directors of the Federal Reserve Bank of Boston. He is past president of the American Economics Association and the Econometric Society, a member of the National Academy of Sciences, a fellow of the British Academy, and a former member of the National Science Board. Professor Solow has received the Nobel Prize in Economics for his theory of growth as well as the National Medal of Science. He has written articles and books on economic growth, macroeconomics, and the theory of unemployment, and occasional reviews in *The New York Review of Books* and *The New Republic*. Some of the books for which he is most noted include *Capital Theory and the Rate of Return* (1963); *Growth Theory: an Exposition* (1970); *Made in America: Regaining the Productive Edge* (with M. Dertouzos, R. Lester, and the MIT Commission on Industrial Productivity, 1989); *The Labor Market as a Social Institution* (1990); and *A Critical Essay on Modern Macroeconomic Theory* (with Frank Hahn, 1995). Professor Solow received bachelor's, master's, and doctoral degrees from Harvard University.

Richard Zeckhauser is the Frank P. Ramsey Professor of Political Economy at the Kennedy School, Harvard University. Professor Zeckhauser is also a research associate at the National Bureau of Economic Research. He created the behavioral finance program at the Kennedy School and has served since then as its faculty chair. Professor Zeckhauser's contributions to the field of behavioral decision and finance include the concepts of status quo bias, barn-door closing, bright-line behavior, betrayal aversion, and denominator blindness. In the practical realm of behavioral decision, he was formerly Victor Niederhoffer's business partner and currently serves as a principal in Equity Resource Investments. Professor Zeckhauser holds a BA, summa cum laude, and a PhD in economics from Harvard.

Contents

CONTINUING
EDUCATION
QUALIFIED ACTIVITY

This publication qualifies for 5 CE credits under the guidelines
of the CFA Institute Continuing Education Program.

Foreword

As I write this foreword, I have been retired for a few days, so postretirement investment and drawdown strategies (asset "decumulation") are very much on my mind. (Decumulation—apparently a made-up word of recent origin, but aren't all words made up?—is the opposite of accumulation.)

Other people in previous generations, and some in the current generation, of retirees have relied on traditional ways of getting by, or of thriving, as they age. The historically earliest ways were "I will let my children support me" or "I will work until I die." These are less than fully satisfying. A fairly large population of lucky or shrewd retirees can say, "I will live on my defined-benefit pension plan." Another group, generally less fortunate but still able to survive, must say, "I will live on Social Security," or whatever the lowest-tier government pension program is in any given country.

Then there is me, and several tens of millions of people like me: "I will live on my savings." (Savings includes defined-contribution plan balances.) But what does it mean to live on your savings? How much can you afford to spend? What should the asset allocation of your investments be, taking into account your home, Social Security and other guaranteed income, and (diminishing) human capital? Should you work part time? What will you do if you run out of money when you are very old? Is there a way to make sure such a catastrophe never happens?

Unfortunately, finance does not give me and my compatriots much of a tool kit to work with. Where is the body of economic theory and empirical work that helps to answer these questions?

The authors here begin valiantly to work toward such a theory, which must address a number of thorny issues. Among these are the role of annuities and other insurance products, sustainable drawdown rates, the effectiveness of using adjustments in one's standard of living as the principal risk control mechanism, and the integration of human capital (income from work) into the postretirement equation. From a public policy standpoint, leaders of government, business, and voluntary associations must consider at what age retirement benefits are to be provided, how large the benefits should be and how quickly they should grow over time, how to fund such benefits, and how to answer such ancillary policy questions as whether phased (partial) retirement should be encouraged or discouraged.

This book is the outgrowth of the second Future of Life-Cycle Saving and Investing conference held at Boston University on 22–24 October 2008. The first such conference, which addressed retirement saving and investment issues at the broadest possible level, was organized by Professor Zvi Bodie of Boston University

©2009 The Research Foundation of CFA Institute

and took place at that location on 25–27 October 2006. It resulted in the precursor to this book, *The Future of Life-Cycle Saving and Investing*, published by the Research Foundation of CFA Institute in 2007.[1]

Professor Bodie also organized the second life-cycle conference. He wisely chose to focus on the part of the retirement equation that has received the least attention and that is thus closest to the frontiers of finance: the behavior and investment strategies of those who have already retired—thus the emphasis on asset decumulation in this book.

As noted in the foreword to the predecessor volume, this series of conferences is distinguished by its avoidance of a finance-only faculty and its inclusion of a varied group of experts, among them actuaries, accountants, lawyers, regulators, nonfinancial corporate executives, union leaders, and trade association representatives. The variety of thinking that comes from bringing such a wide array of people together is invaluable.

Through our sponsorship of this series of conferences and our publication of the associated books, we hope not only to stimulate thinking but also to promote real change. This book showcases finance at its most practical, and we are especially pleased to present it.

Laurence B. Siegel
Research Director
Research Foundation of CFA Institute

---

[1]Zvi Bodie, Dennis McLeavey, and Laurence Siegel, eds., *The Future of Life-Cycle Saving and Investing* (Charlottesville, VA: Research Foundation of CFA Institute, 2007): www.cfapubs.org/toc/rf/2007/2007/3.

Overview

Zvi Bodie

Norman and Adele Barron Professor of Management
Boston University
Boston

In October 2008, about 150 economists, actuaries, research scientists, investment managers, and advisers met for two days at Boston University to analyze the most pressing financial issues facing the "Boomer" generation in developed nations with aging populations. The conference took place just before the election of Barack Obama as U.S. President, and the global economy was in the worst financial crisis since the Great Depression. The retirement savings, home values, and stock portfolios of U.S. families were hard hit, and the short-run outlook for employment and growth was not good. Most of the invited speakers and other participants addressed issues related to long-run trends of a society in which the elderly population is becoming a significantly larger proportion of the total. In this book, we present the parts of the conference that we believe will be of greatest interest to decision makers in government and business as well as professional consultants, advisers, and educators.

The 2008 conference was the second in the series titled "The Future of Life-Cycle Saving and Investing." The first conference was held in 2006, sponsored jointly by the Research Foundation of CFA Institute and the Federal Reserve Bank of Boston.[1] The 2008 conference had seven sponsoring organizations: the Research Foundation of CFA Institute, the Federal Reserve Bank of Boston, the Employee Benefit Research Institute (EBRI), the Network for Studies on Pensions, Aging and Retirement (Netspar), the Professional Risk Managers' International Association (PRMIA), the Retirement Income Industry Association (RIIA), and the Society of Actuaries (SOA).[2]

In the opening address, Professor Peter Diamond set the stage for subsequent discussions by describing the major demographic and economic trends affecting aging populations globally and by analyzing the implications for retirement and pension systems. Around the world, both public and private pension plans have failed to adapt to long-term demographic trends: increasing life expectancy, decreasing birth rates, and lower labor force participation rates. The resultant increase in the ratio of retirees to working-age population makes existing institutional arrangements

---

[1]Selected webcasts of the presentations from the 2006 conference (www.cfawebcasts.org/cpe/what_pac.cfm?test_id=183) and 2008 conference (www.cfawebcasts.org/cpe/what_pac.cfm?test_id=215) are on the CFA Institute website.

[2]Details of the 2008 conference are on the Boston University conference website (http://management.bu.edu/exec/elc/Lifecycle/2008/index.shtml).

unsustainable without major reforms. Diamond analyzes four main courses of action: higher contributions, lower benefits, later retirement, and policies designed to increase national output in order to afford a more generous pension system.

A major highlight of the conference was a panel discussion among three Nobel laureates in economics (Paul Samuelson, Robert Solow, and Robert C. Merton) on the subject of what retirement means to me. The moderator, Paul Solman, posed a series of questions to the panelists:

- How do you spend, or plan to spend, your time in retirement?
- How do you invest your retirement savings?
- What advice do you have for the younger generation about how to prepare for retirement?

Their answers made clear that these three economists have not stopped working or even slowed down as they have aged. They have different investment portfolios, but they all have similar advice for the young—find a job that you love.[3]

There were six other conference sessions, four of which are included in this volume:

- Health Care and Assisted Living for the Elderly
- Phased Retirement
- How Older People Behave
- The Future of Pensions and Retirement in Europe

Each of these sessions, although important and worthy in its own right, was designed to be part of a mosaic backdrop that describes the current state of retirement planning (both theoretically and practically) as well as the challenges for designing structures and solutions that meet retirees' needs.

Health Care and Assisted Living for the Elderly

This panel discussed the current status of the health and fitness of the elderly population in the United States and the prospects for the future. First, what can today's elderly individuals expect in terms of living on their own or in independent living, assisted living, or in nursing homes? And who pays for this care—private saving, voluntary insurance, Medicaid, or Medicare? Second, how much do today's Baby Boomers need to save to hedge against growing health care costs? And do they need to save to hedge against such contingencies as a lengthy stay in a nursing home? Key factors in answering this latter question are what is the quality of institutional care (particularly for Medicaid patients) and how much support might come from children of the elderly? Third, what are the prospects for long-term care insurance—how good are the policies, and how can long-term care be improved? Finally, what are some of the imaginative innovations in residential arrangements (such as the naturally occurring retirement communities) and their prospects for diffusion across the United States?

---

[3] The entire 90-minute session can be viewed online at www.bu.edu/phpbin/buniverse/videos/view/?id=260.

Phased Retirement

Among the most important factors in determining how much one needs to save for retirement are the age at which one plans to retire from full-time work and the extent to which one continues to work part time after that. Delaying retirement allows one to put aside more savings and also reduces the number of years over which one must stretch those savings. Extending one's labor force participation beyond retirement from a full-time career job, whether through phased retirement from that job or through a new, flexible "bridge job," allows one to supplement retirement income and reduces the amount of savings needed to maintain preretirement living standards. The panel addressed the role that delayed and phased retirement should—and is likely to—play in households' life-cycle planning.

How Older People Behave

Making prudent financial decisions for retirement is fraught with difficulties. This session discussed both preretirement and postretirement behavior—noting the common mistakes and decision pitfalls of individuals and also some of the limitations of professional financial advice. Among the questions examined were the following:

- What innovations can improve financial planning for retirement?
- How active a role (heavy a burden) should the individual bear?
- Would paternalistic guidelines or constraints induce better decisions?
- What is the division of labor between retirement "ends" (the individual's stated goals and preferences) and financial "means"?
- What role should public policy play?

The Future of Pensions and Retirement in Europe

The first paper in this session examined Dutch collective pension schemes, which offer a third way between corporate defined-benefit schemes and individual defined-contribution schemes. The members of the fund are the risk bearers, and the funds manage risk aimed at providing an adequate income level during retirement at low costs. Is this the structure other European countries will follow? Is it the structure that the United States and the rest of the world should follow?

Conclusion

The eclectic portfolio of topics in these sessions illustrates well that life-cycle saving and investing is a multidisciplinary endeavor that challenges financial advisers and product providers alike. It is perhaps instructive to observe that if life-cycle solutions are difficult for financial professionals to identify, how much more difficult must it be for ordinary individuals navigating a complicated landscape? We hope that this conference helps usher in a new era of sophisticated financial advice and products for individuals either in retirement or saving to retire.

Nobel Laureate Panel Discussion: What Retirement Means to Me

Paul Samuelson
Institute Professor Emeritus
Massachusetts Institute of Technology
Cambridge, Massachusetts

Robert Solow
Institute Professor Emeritus
Massachusetts Institute of Technology
Cambridge, Massachusetts

Robert Merton
John and Natty McArthur University Professor
Harvard Business School
Boston

In a rare event, three Nobel prize winners in economics discuss retirement: theirs, that of the current generation approaching retirement, and that of future generations. In particular, their comments address the impact of the current financial crisis on everyone's retirement aspirations.

Solman: Something like 10 percent of all living Nobel laureate economists are sitting right here, and following some introductory remarks by perhaps the wisest person I have ever met, Paul Samuelson, I am going to pose four questions to them.

Samuelson: I ruminate often about proposed advice on how people should save for their retirement nest eggs. Some believe that everything should be in TIPS (U.S. Treasury Inflation-Protected Securities), but I paddle my own canoe. I am going to trot out a few heresies, and each one comes with a story.

One open conjecture of mine could be that the same ideal portfolio might be ideal for investors on different geographical continents. Once upon a time, I served as a TIAA–CREF (Teachers Insurance and Annuity Association–College Retirement Equities Fund) trustee on the CREF Finance Committee, and I got a vituperative letter from a TIAA participant. He had moved to New Zealand for a tenured job in a university English department, and when he asked to transfer his TIAA accumulation to that place, TIAA said no. In reply, I explained that had he

---

Editor's Note: *Paul Solman served as moderator for this session.*

been in CREF, he could soon get his contribution and transfer it. But then I went on to explain that "as TIAA is currently structured, no accurate quote of its worth, its marked-to-market price, is possible." Keep in mind that this subject is very hot right now. And continuing to quote from my letter: "At this time, its nominal book value is above its best estimated, realistic, net asset value. If one rat leaves the ship with more than his share of its cargo, that would be unfair to all the other rats." I could have left it there. But big-mouth Samuelson went on to argue, "I am not sure that a New Zealander ought not to have today about the same global portfolio as an American or Japanese ought to have."

Heretical? Maybe not in 2010.

Many analysts argue that when you average over many investment periods, so favorable are the long-run returns of stocks that while you are still young, you should borrow substantially to hold large positions in stocks and you should do so because some kind of "stochastic dominance" is supposed to justify it.

Now, when I read such things, my eyebrows arch upwards. I think I have written 27 articles rebutting this idea—with at least one article completely in one-syllable words, except for the word "syllable" itself. It smacks of what I call the "Milton Friedman fallacy." When that sage was a TIAA trustee before me, he believed that investing for a large number of future periods did, by some law of large numbers, mandate becoming more risk tolerant.

The Milton Friedman fallacy is a simple one. Also called the Kelly criterion, it leads to the conclusion that, in contrast to utility theory, one should always maximize the geometric mean.[1] It is the same as the 1738 Daniel Bernoulli conjecture that if you have a duel with your brother-in-law and you are faced with a stationary probability process—stationary through time—going to the geometric mean is the way to win.[2] Being second in investing, unlike being second in dueling, is good, however, and very few attain it.

The ideas that I have been criticizing do not shrivel up and die. They always come back. Consider the following: Most people, I think—but I stand ready to be corrected—have increasing relative risk tolerance as their wealth increases. So, a John D. Rockefeller can be more risk tolerant—that is, more nearly risk neutral—than I can be. This situation is not inevitable, but I think it is true for most people. Yet, recently, I received an abstract for a paper in which a Yale economist and a Yale law school professor advise the world that when you are young and you have many years ahead of you, you should borrow heavily, invest in stocks on margin, and make a lot of money. I want to remind them, with a well-chosen counterexample: I always quote

---

[1] The Kelly criterion is a formula used to determine the optimal size of a series of bets; it was described by J.L. Kelly, Jr., in 1956.

[2] See *Specimen theoriae novae de mensura sortis* [*Exposition of a New Theory on the Measurement of Risk*] (1738); English translation in *Econometrica*, vol. 22 (1954):23–36.

from Warren Buffett (that wise, wise man from Nebraska) that in order to succeed, you must first survive. People who leverage heavily when they are very young do not realize that the sky is the limit of what they could lose and from that point on, they would be knocked out of the game.

Merton: I would like to respond to the idea of the geometric mean. Keep in mind that I am a Rational Man—with big R and big M. I used to go on cruises during the summer. Needing something to do, I would find myself in a casino. To be social, I had to play something. So, I would put a bunch of $5 chips in one pocket and go to the roulette wheel. I played "double your bet," in which I put five on something and if I won, I took the winnings off and put them in the other pocket. If I lost, I doubled. Then, if I eventually won, I would get back all the money I had lost.

So, one time, I was judiciously playing, and it was very crowded around the table. And I had a run. I was playing red, and red kept coming up, and I kept piling up chips. Then, I noticed that someone else must have been playing another strategy because right next to my chip, on that same red, was this pile of chips growing because someone had simply let it all ride. I was taking in all the chips. And suddenly, I got an inspiration. At the same time, the croupier looked over, and said, "Who owns these chips?" Because the pile was getting pretty high. Nobody moved. And I realized that, by accident, I had left an extra chip out there; I had been winning without knowing it (using the let-it-ride strategy), and the unclaimed pile of chips was, in fact, mine. The moral of this story is that it is better to be lucky than smart. Now, what does all of this have to do with retirement?

Solman: Thank you both, I think, for introducing the topic. I have four questions that I would like you to address: First, when do you intend to retire? Second, when should *I* retire; that is, when should somebody who is 64 years old retire? Third, is there a retirement savings crisis in the United States? And with the fourth question, we will get to the younger people in the audience. So, Robert Solow, when do you plan to retire, or have you?

Solow: I have retired, and I can tell you exactly when and why I retired. I was a member of the first cohort of academics that had no compulsory retirement age. I could have stayed on even to now, but I went to the provost of MIT (Massachusetts Institute of Technology) and asked him, "Would you like to get your hands on my salary?" And he sort of salivated visibly, so I said, "I'll tell you what. I will retire as if I had to retire at age 70, provided you give my department an extra assistant professor." And he said, "It's a deal." So, I retired. I get a pension instead of a salary.

Well, I actually did think about the topic—what does retirement mean to me—and I have an answer to it. If you think about retirement in the sense of a time-and-motion study, what does one actually do? I find that I am more active than I want to be. And I am conscious of the fact that a good psychologist would probably say, "How active you are really tells you how active you want to be." But I do not feel that way. I feel that events, circumstances, keep me doing more than I want to do.

And I think I understand why. I had a long, charmed academic life. In that long academic life, I accumulated, not obligations, but sentiments, attachments. I find that I am invited to do things by a lot of friends, including former students, for whom I have respectful and warm feelings—Zvi Bodie, for example, for this conference. A student who is now the head of a department in Florida invited me to go down there and lecture in the spring. I was flattered and thought my wife and I could go visit friends, so I said I would. I even, for heaven's sake, agreed to give a talk that I do not particularly want to give because a student of James Tobin's asked me to. I remember Tobin fondly from the Council of Economic Advisers in the early 1960s.

Sometimes I get paid and sometimes not. If the occasion is at a university that I think does not have a lot of money, I do not take the pay. I do it because it seems like the right thing to do.

And sometimes, of course, I luck into something that is really fascinating and useful, like my relationship with the Russell Sage Foundation, where I am the Robert K. Merton Scholar.

So, I find myself doing things out of sentiment that are not exactly the way I would have foreseen or wanted if I had sat down and planned my retirement years. I get to do things that I think are valuable and interesting, but I still wonder when I am going to wake up in the morning and say to myself, "You have nothing to do?" That is what I would really like. I would like to wake up in the morning, some morning, and say, "There is nothing on my list." I don't know when it will happen.

Solman: And you, Professor Merton, you are 64, my age exactly, so when should you and I retire?

Merton: I do not know what I will decide. I want to do it sometime, but right now, I feel very blessed doing what I am doing. I have had a wonderful life so far, and I like what I am doing. I cannot imagine putting on green pants and a pink shirt and banging a ball around Pebble Beach or something like that. Of course, I would have to be able to afford it, and that is hypothetical after what has happened. But I look for a reason *not* to do that. So, I actually do not have any intention of retiring as long as my brain works and my health is OK.

Of course, I can talk about only how I feel right now. I have learned a lot from the two men on this panel, so when Bob Solow said he likes the idea of having nothing on the list, I made a note of that. And I thought, hmmm, I could change my mind.

Solman: All three of you have such an enormous amount of human capital that you may not be like the rest of us when it comes to the optimal time to retire. Your services will always be in demand as long as you are in good health and *compos mentis*. Do you, as a result not only of your enjoyment of your work but also the fact that you have enormous human capital, have a lot of disability insurance?

Merton: I have a fair amount, but also I have precautionary savings in the event that something threatens my human capital. Of course, if my brain turns to mush, I will not know what is going on, so I do not want to insure too much.

In thinking about retirement, what we really need to do is consider all our assets. In this current financial crisis, almost everything I own went down—house, equities, and all that sort of thing. I thought the one thing we could be very secure about when a flight to quality occurs is something like TIPS. They are backed by the full faith and credit of the U.S. government. So, they must have rallied big. I thought they were the one bright spot, but it turned out that I lost 8–12 percent, depending on the bonds, in the middle of a flight to quality. So, I managed to find the perfectly secure investment, and it still managed to go down. My portfolio is almost perfect. You just need to short it.

Human capital is clearly going to be very important in the future. Bob Solow made the voluntary decision not to take advantage of the anti-age-discrimination law that would have allowed him to stay on indefinitely. That decision was a *conscious* decision. People must consider what retirement will bring them, and human capital is an important element of that decision.

It is depressing when you think you want a life annuity. Say you are 65 years old and do not have anybody else in the world you care to leave money to and you ask, "How much can I get for so much money?" According to Zvi Bodie, the depressing number is 6 percent. So, if you want $50,000 per year, you have to have about $800,000 invested. You think you are pretty well off, and then you see what kind of return you are going to get and where you are going to live. It underlines how valuable human capital is. Look at how much cash it would take to generate what you generate yourself with your own human capital. And if you generate that cash by doing what you like to do, rather than hitting balls around a golf course, you have a good deal.

You can increase your return in a couple of ways. One is to keep costs low. That element you can control. The other is to make the most efficient use of your assets. What would that be in light of where we are now—with the decline in everything? I believe, for most assets, it is a permanent decline. I do not think this decline is a liquidity event, although it contains a lot of liquidity problems. A few weeks ago, I said on a panel that I thought we had lost $4 trillion in residential real estate in the United States alone. I got a lot of e-mails telling me, no, the government says it is a quarter of that. The government numbers are wrong—not wrong, exactly, but applied only to a select number of houses. Warren Buffett said the figure is $4 trillion plus. I do not know whether we are down $4 trillion or $5 trillion in real estate. The U.S. stock market is down $8 trillion to $9 trillion. So, the sum from those two identifiable sources is already 85 percent of one year's U.S. GDP, with no offsetting gain.

The good news is that most people are still living in the same house. So, they have less wealth, but they do not need as much. Your house is a great hedge.

What that statement misses out on in relation to this conference is the role of the house's residual value in financing retirement. And this aspect is going to be important because a lot of money, a lot of wealth, is gone that we have no reason to think will come back.

In response, I think we need a lot of efficiency in the tools used for retirement. For those of us engaged in this area, finding these tools is both a huge challenge and a great opportunity. If we did not have enough reason before, we certainly do now to come up with reverse mortgages that are efficient, instead of the kinds we have now. And we have reasons to recognize a host of other elements that can make a difference in people's retirements. Two years ago, General Motors Corporation got rid of its DB (defined-benefit) plan and replaced it with a DC (defined-contribution) plan, a 401(k) plan, as did many other companies. GM announced on 23 October 2008 that it is no longer making contributions to its 401(k) plans. I suspect it will not be alone.

Samuelson: For efficient asset allocation, the most important issue that vexes the minds of people on the finance committee of the National Academy of Sciences is the following. The record for market timers who try to buy when stocks are low and sell when stocks are high is awful. Knowing when to sell is not so hard, but timers do not know when to get back in. Moreover, in normal cycles, when the time comes to go back into the market, everything typically moves very, very fast. What should we think when somebody as wise as Alan Greenspan says that today's market is a once-in-a-century event? Should we still, in that case, take in no sail at all? The decision is hard because for such an event, history teaches no lessons. We deal in nonstationary time series. To neglect the bits of wisdom that history does tell, however, would be crazy. If you choose to sleep better now, maybe you will regret it, but maybe we are in an extremely unusual perfect storm and the rules that are optimal under normal conditions are not optimal now.

Solman: I interviewed Professor Samuelson in 1984 for a newspaper, and he suggested an asset allocation of 50 percent stocks, 25 percent long-duration bonds, and 25 percent short-duration bonds or cash. He stated that an investor with this allocation would do as well as any money manager and would sleep better at night. If I were interviewing each of you now, what would you suggest as the ideal asset allocation?

Samuelson: I think what I was giving you was the TIAA–CREF mix at that time. It did not have as much foreign investments as it should have had then and as it would have now.

Merton: In my retirement accounts, I am in TIPS, and I have a global index fund that has all-in expenses of 8 bps. I will not tell you which firm it is with, but you would be surprised. At least it was a surprise to me, but if they are willing to do that deal, it is fine with me. Also, I have one hedge fund that gives me some exposure in unusual areas. Until eight months ago, I was in a real estate fund, commercial real estate, and then I simply became very nervous because it seemed to be valued on the basis of appraisals. I would wonder, is that correct? I got nervous because the real estate fund was going up every day like a bank account—except one with a very nice interest rate. I thought maybe marked-to-market values might be better data than appraisals in times when you are not sure, which is why I was nervous. If someone has based the value on historical price, the evidence is that that price no longer holds.

Also, of course, I own residential real estate, and I need not comment on that. So, my asset allocation is pretty ordinary.

I had some municipal bonds. I thought, well, I have Massachusetts municipal bonds, and I know Massachusetts is not going to go broke. However, municipalities are in a great deal of trouble. I do not know what the bankruptcy law is for municipalities, but if it is similar to corporate law, I do worry about it. We are well aware of the corporate pension underfunding issues, but given the labor contracts of municipalities, I suspect we will be talking a lot more about pension underfunding at municipalities. Moreover, I believe, it is virtually impossible for municipalities to borrow right now. At some point in the future, this problem could be fixed, but I worry that the municipalities will decide the only way to get out of their labor contracts is what the airlines did and will go bankrupt. Maybe they cannot legally go bankrupt, but if they can, that route could be chosen by more and more municipalities if one does it successfully and others follow. This example shows how looking at historical default rates may not help you. It is a little bit like when I drive on the Massachusetts Turnpike. I think of myself as a very conservative driver, but I like to drive sometimes a little faster than the speed limit. So, say I am driving and looking in the rearview mirror to see if there is anybody back there that I should be concerned about, and I realize I am driving 100 feet a second while looking in the rearview mirror. That works very well, as we all know, as long as the road in front of you is like the one behind you.

Samuelson: Why would one not be interested in a Harvard University, 28-year bond at par that pays 5 percent? What credit risk would you see?

Merton: Oh, well, Harvard is OK, but I was talking about municipalities.

Samuelson: They are doubly tax exempt.

Merton: Aha, well, now for those of you who live in Massachusetts, I deserve some applause, at least appreciation, because I finally got a real piece of investment advice out of Paul Samuelson!

Samuelson: I did not say I bought any.

Merton: That is OK; you pointed it out. It sounds pretty good to me. I think everyone should write that down right now.

Solman: Third question: Is there a retirement savings crisis in the United States?

Samuelson: Yes, and it will expand because a lot of contracts that people think are sound will be reneged on. There will also have been tremendous losses. Fifteen years ago, a prominent economist, who was very young, predicted a forthcoming bad housing market. He did so because of the great number of retiring Baby Boomers he could foresee. He had it wrong because he did not realize that, without the contrivance of money, housing is the main instrument, the main carry-through from generation to generation. If he had waited maybe 12–15 more years, the mechanism he was talking about would have become operative. Certainly, there will be a savings crisis.

I believe the election in November will change the government, but the crisis may result in an overreaction instead of the country going back to the perfect Samuelson center. Think of the moral hazard problems if the government ends up owning most of the economy.

Solman: Do you think we are headed for the Scandinavianization of the U.S. economy?

Samuelson: Well, that might be a compliment because in Scandinavia, not in Spain, you do not have to have a ticket collected on the trams. A certain historical honesty is getting undermined. Let me tell a little story. I once met the most eminent Brazilian economist. At the time, he was almost as old as I am now, and he had written either a daily column or a weekly column for the previous 35 or 40 years. I said to him, "In all of your lifetime, there has been galloping hyperinflation in Brazil." He did not demur. I said, "How come there has never been a good common stock market with indexed common stocks to serve as an inflation hedge?" He said, "Well, I will tell you why. It would be ridiculous to buy those common stocks—because the companies will cheat you." At the time, I thought how wonderful it was to be in a country like the United States, where you can trust the accounting.

But in the past eight years, we have moved into exactly that kind of Brazilian situation. "Operating earnings"—that concept is the greatest invention for cheating in every possible way. Even for Jack Welch, the great, admired General Electric man, his principal function was to make sure earnings always appeared to be growing smoothly whether they were or not. "Operating earnings" are a rigged calculation.

I hope that with centrist democrats, including local Congressman Barney Frank, we may get to a point where more honest relationships exist in our systems of accounts.

Solow: Well, I cannot produce that kind of stream of consciousness, but sure, there is a retirement crisis, in the sense that a lot of wealth—putative wealth—has disappeared that retirees had counted on. I would like to mention that I had not known this news about GM, just like that, turning off its contributions to 401(k) plans. So, it is not only current retirees but also retirees down the road who face a crisis. And certainly, whatever happens over the next 12, 24, or 36 months is not going to restore the status quo ante. So, a lot of revision of expectations about retirement incomes is needed, and I am sure it is happening.

Merton: I mentioned at the outset the loss in wealth. It is real. Nothing can be done about that loss; people will have to revise their expectations. But we need to focus on what we can do, not what we cannot do.

One of the issues of the switch from DB plans to DC plans, which have, in truth, become the norm, is that the maximum contribution limits have gone up only a little. As we all know, we used to have a retirement system in the United States in which workers had Social Security, many people had DB plans, and the wealthier workers had 401(k) plans as a supplement, an add-on. But now, the DC plans have to perform the function for all employees that the DB plans used to play. That change has a lot to do with asset allocation in the employee's DC plan, which must be different from when that plan complemented a DB component.

Another issue is how people are going to save enough when their maximum limits are more or less the same as they used to be, but now, their contributions are required to do, in a sense, double duty. If you are over the age of 50, the limit is only $22,000 a year in 2009, and it is even less if you are younger.

Solman: Some here are frowning because that amount is so much, given what most people's normal cash flow is. The median family income is about $50,000.

Merton: I am thinking more about the reality of people not having saved in DC plans since they were 23. Because the DC plans have been capped, a lot of people over 50 are finding themselves with totally inadequate savings. The mean balance is about $66,000.

If you want a list of what can go wrong, one element is, as I mentioned, that municipalities may not be able to honor their pension commitments. Another element, which I alluded to, is commercial mortgages, which have not yet become a focus. With all the contractions of financial firms—and who knows how many hedge funds will go out of business but possibly a third to half of them—certain cities are going to be left with a lot of vacant commercial real estate. I have not seen that aspect reflected in the data, so that could be another worry. And then, of course, $2 trillion or so has been lost in pension funds, so you can imagine what that is doing to those previously overfunded plans. And consider the eventual effect on the Pension Benefit Guaranty Corporation. Not all these disasters are going to happen, but we have plenty to worry about and work on.

Solman: What retirement advice would you give to somebody who is 20 years old?

Samuelson: Learn to use your computer. Learn your calculus. Learn the Black–Scholes option-pricing model.

Solow: For a 20-year-old, retirement is a long way off. Earn and save.

Merton: Earn and save sounds pretty good to me.

Solman: Should that person be investing in stocks?

Merton: Sure, sure. Recently, even in the middle of this crisis, I was at a bank board meeting, where they had plenty of other things to talk about, but the first question that came up from these well-educated, smart people was, do you think this is the bottom? I bring up this question because it is making a statement about expected value. You might think the first question would be, How much risk do we have right now? But they were looking toward the expected rate of return.

Economic models have an error term. But the error term is not an important element of the model's forecast. One branch of economics is different, the branch of finance. Finance is all about the error term. What we think about is not so much what the expected outcome is—it is what it is—but, rather, what are the various paths that can occur, the risks. And then the contingent question is, If a particular path occurs, what should we do about it? Working back from that question, we deal with what we should do about it today. So, I think your question has less to do with the riskiness in the market than with whether now is a good time to be getting into the market.

Yes, 20-year-olds and 30-year-olds ought to be investing some amount in equities, in ownership of assets in the economy and, preferably, international as well as domestic. And yes, the market may go a lot lower.

By the way, at one point in the last two weeks or so, you could write credit protection for the U.S. Treasury, in which you are guaranteeing obligations of the U.S. Treasury (although not in dollars because it has to be in a different currency). You would not be buying a credit default swap; you would be offering to sell one. For example, to sell protection, insurance, you could sell a guarantee of the U.S. Treasury for, say, 10 years at 30 bps a year. If you wrote that insurance for $1 million, you would get $3,000 a year for the next 10 years.

So, if you thought the U.S. Treasury would not default, you could sell that insurance.

Of course, scenarios other than the breakdown of the economy as we know it might trigger making good on that insurance. A "credit event" might be, for example, lifting the debt ceiling, not actually going broke. The point is that people often say, "Well, there is no problem with U.S. Treasury securities because if the United States defaults on its debt, that is the end of the financial system globally, so anything you hold is up for grabs and it does not matter." I can imagine a circumstance in the future when a huge amount of U.S. debt is held outside the United States—China, in particular—where that country decides to exert the kind of influence that the United States did with the United Kingdom and France at the time of the Suez Crisis in 1956. That is, suppose China says, "We do not like what you are doing, and we want you to stop." And we refuse. And China says, "OK, then we are going to sell all the U.S. debt we hold tomorrow." They are just going to dump it on the market. I think people would say, "No way. This is national security. We are not going to let another country dictate our national policy, so you know what? We are going to default. We will not pay them, but we will take care of everybody else, just like we are doing now, in a different way." This scenario is a very remote possibility; please do not hear this as a forecast. I am suggesting that we have seen from experience that trigger events can be realistic things that you had never thought about, not the end of the world.

Samuelson: Dickens wrote *A Tale of Two Cities*, and I am going to spin a "Tale of Two Persons." One of them is Joseph Kennedy, Sr. He made his big money not by selling Scotch legally or illegally but by selling the U.S. stock market short, year after year, in 1930, 1931, 1932, and the first part of 1933. Then, in 1945, he put it all into buying the Merchandise Mart in Chicago, the biggest building in the world, which he bought at that time for almost a song.

The second person is perhaps the greatest American economist who ever lived, Yale Professor Irving Fisher. Irving Fisher was the son of a poor Protestant minister. However, he married into a chemical industry fortune. Then, in 1919, he invented a visible filing system, and he made a bundle of money from it. Throughout the 1920s, he was heavily in the bull market on margin. Just before the huge market fall, he was saying that prices still had not caught up with real values and should go much higher. On 21 October 1929, he said that the market was "only shaking out the lunatic fringe." Then, and I think this story is literally true, he was in Mussolini's office when a call came from New York. His assistant told Fisher they had a margin call that they could not meet. And suddenly, the fortune was gone. So, he went back to the drawing boards and studied more minutely. And he said, "My original ideas were wrong, but I have now worked it out. Things are so cheap that this is a great time to invest." Young people might have taken up that idea and invested. But he was wrong again: The market fell as much after that time as it did before. Now which guy was right? Old Joe Kennedy or Irving Fisher?

Question and Answer Session

Paul Samuelson
Robert Solow
Robert Merton

Question: I would like to raise a policy question with the panel. I think that at this time, economists need to come up with the best policy answers to help the country and the world. I may be a little bit more upbeat than Professor Samuelson. I believe we had a *generational* imbalance in policy that had to be corrected. You could view this financial correction as a transfer from wealthy older people and Baby Boomers to the younger generation, who now are able to buy up these assets at lower prices—if we do not all panic. Unfortunately, we have a collapse of confidence, but if we didn't, if there were no budget constraints on the young people, no high unemployment, and no empty buildings, we would have the same real wealth. It is just that the older people hold less, and the younger people have some gains. The gains are subtle and hard to see, but they are offsetting capital gains. There is no aggregate income effect.

Moreover, we need the government to make a real statement about confidence in this economy. Taking history as a lesson, I think the economy at some point will recover. So, here is my question. We have had this decline in stock values and house values. The government is coming in and buying up bank stocks. Is this the time for the Treasury to borrow (that is, to take freshly created money, freshly created Treasury bills) and invest in the stock market broadly to support the market? It would be on behalf of the younger generations, who are too afraid or out of work or can't afford to buy up the stock market, to keep the taxes on the next generation lower than they would otherwise be. Moreover, if the Treasury doesn't do this, the Chinese or the Japanese or the Koreans may do it. They may take their Treasury securities and swap them for U.S. stocks at these bargain-basement prices.

Such a move is not something I would recommend in standard conditions, but these are not standard times.

Samuelson: I am full of sensible heresies. How do you think the United States got out of that depression in President Franklin Roosevelt's time? How do you think Germany got out of it in pernicious Adolf Hitler's time? The Germans inherited about the same level of unemployment—at least one third of the work force. And both got out of it in about the same number of years, by 1939.

Well, somebody invented helicopters. And somebody went to the printing press and printed off millions and billions of legal tender, and then those helicopters flew over the poor, rural regions and the poor areas of cities, where there wasn't a problem of whether the money was going to be saved or spent. (I am speaking figuratively of course.)

The helicopter runs in the United States were not a Federal Reserve operation, and the reason is that in the first week following Roosevelt's inauguration, every bank in the country was closed down. And only the good banks were allowed to reopen. In Berlin, Wisconsin, the bank run by Will Crawford was the only bank that was allowed to reopen. The reason was that Crawford knew every borrower who had a mortgage in Berlin, Wisconsin, population 4,106 at the time. And he knew better than they did what they could afford to borrow. He didn't go out and start making new loans. He acquired more Treasury certificates, which had a yield of essentially zero.

So, in effect, we got out of the Great Depression by deficit spending. E.C. Brown provided the best analysis of the deficit spending and the putative effects under the most plausible models.[3] There were no miracles.

Some of you will remember Professor John Williams, one of my mentors at Harvard. He was a Will Rogers kind of guy, and he lost a bundle in the Great Depression. That is, he was not a good Depression economist. He said in the classroom, "I would not make any loan on the safest investment." That was a widespread opinion and behavior, and I'm sure it was matched in Germany and other places. So, breaking out of the Depression had to be done by different means. I think something similar is going to happen now.

Solow: The purpose of the Treasury buying the stock is to own common stock in U.S. corporations on behalf of 30-year-olds? I don't really regard that as an intelligible function of the federal government. In my view, a vote is a vote, regardless of its age. I think the federal government would be better advised to be thinking about supporting the real economy rather than supporting the stock market.

Merton: I think that if you do open market operations to stimulate private-sector investments, then taking equity positions directly is better than trying to do it by manipulating interest rates.

For that purpose, I would say the Treasury should not buy stock; it should do it with the equivalent of futures, which would be a much cleaner, much better way, and it would take on the risk without having to deal with any of the other matters, such as proxy voting.

The questioner made an assumption that these stocks are at bargain-basement prices. I believe six months ago, people also thought a lot of stocks were at bargain-basement prices. If I could *know* prices were at the bottom, I think it would be great for the Treasury to buy up the market. We could fund the whole budget that way. I'm willing to invest.

---

[3]E.C. Brown, "Fiscal Policy in the Thirties: A Reappraisal," *American Economic Review*, vol. 46, no. 5 (December 1956):857–879.

Something comes up in trading, however, for which I don't have the answer. Suppose you're a trader and you're sophisticated; you have all the tools. You analyzed some securities or markets, and you decided to buy one, but after you bought it the price went down further, so now it looks even better. One forecast is that it will mean revert, so you should buy even more of it at bargain-basement prices. Some traders do that and succeed; they must have ice water in their veins to do it and stick to their theory about what the security is worth. They are not spooked or fearful. Unfortunately, at times, the prices do not revert, and they are wiped out. Then, they lament why they took so much risk. I don't know how to tell anyone how to make that decision other than, do the best you can. I haven't seen any theory that helps with that decision. You can use all the tools you have in the world, but in the end, you simply have to make a judgment.

I bring that up because if we accept the predicate that everything is cheap, we could follow a number of policies. The question is, what if the market isn't cheap? The government already has an investment in the economy through the tax base. It would be doubling up with leverage. Now, where have we heard that being done? So, the end would be the same—either a great trade or a disaster. And if it's a disaster, all of us will say, "How could you let the federal government leverage up in the same way that the private sector is being criticized for?"

If we have reasons to do open market operations to try to jog the markets, although I don't believe we do, I could see doing that using futures. I don't think it's a wise idea to do it using individual stocks.

On the Future of Pensions and Retirements

Peter Diamond
Institute Professor and Professor of Economics
Massachusetts Institute of Technology
Cambridge, Massachusetts

The global pension crisis has arisen because both public and private pension plans have failed to adapt to long-term demographic trends, such as increasing life expectancy, decreasing birth rates, and lower labor force participation rates. Pension plan reform has largely taken the path of reducing benefits, but other solutions to the pension crisis are available.

Admittedly, in the current economic environment, "pension crisis" has come to mean the severe drop in the market values of pension and retirement accounts. In this presentation, however, I use the term "pension crisis" in its traditional sense—meaning that problems exist around the world in the reconciliation of contributions paid into retirement systems with benefits paid out.

Historical Perspective

A number of demographic trends matter for global pension and retirement system demands. Life expectancy, mortality rate, birth rate, migration, labor force participation rate, and retirement age—all have the potential to affect private and public pension systems.

Tremendous progress has been made in life expectancy as humankind has made significant social, technological, and health care advances over time. The survival curves depicted in **Figure 1** range from an estimate of survival rates in the Stone Age at the bottom of the graph to survival rates in the United States in 1998 at the top of the graph. Needless to say, the difference is quite dramatic; improving longevity is a social goal that has been around for a long time.

Although substantial improvements have been made in infant and childhood mortality, they do not have a direct impact on pensions but, rather, combine with fertility and migration in affecting later labor supply. Adult mortality, however, does have a direct impact, and for many years, life expectancy has been lengthening in many countries. In France, Italy, Sweden, and the United States, for example, the life expectancy of men and women at age 21—roughly the average age people enter the workforce—has gone from 40–45 years in 1900 to roughly 55 years in 2000; a similar upward-sloping trend occurred throughout the previous century.

Figure 1. Survival Curves for Select Historical Periods

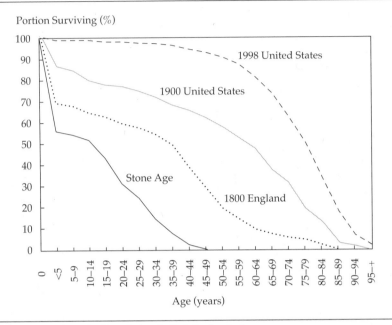

Source: Based on data from the Foundation for Infinite Survival.

The remaining life expectancy at retirement age, approximately age 65, has—like life expectancy in general—increased over the last century. The expectation for living after age 65 has gone from 10–13 years in 1900 to 16–18 years in 2000 in the same four countries. Future mortality rates are always uncertain and are currently being hotly debated among demographers, actuaries, and economists. Uncertainty about future mortality rates is a prime reason that benefit systems should be indexed to changes in actual mortality rather than legislating changes based on anticipated improvements in mortality.

Accompanying the long-term positive trend in U.S. life expectancy has been a long-term negative trend in birth rates, interrupted briefly by the baby boom following World War II and remaining roughly flat since reaching the pre-baby boom level, as shown in **Figure 2**. Fertility rates have also declined sharply over the latter part of the 20th century in many countries, both developed and developing.

To reflect both fertility and mortality rates, one can calculate what is called the old-age dependency ratio, or the population older than age 65 divided by the population between ages 20 and 64. **Figure 3** illustrates how the ratio has steadily increased in France, Italy, Sweden, and the United States since the beginning of the 20th century and also shows a steep projected growth rate as the Baby Boomers

Figure 2.   Total Fertility Rate in the United States, 1810–2070

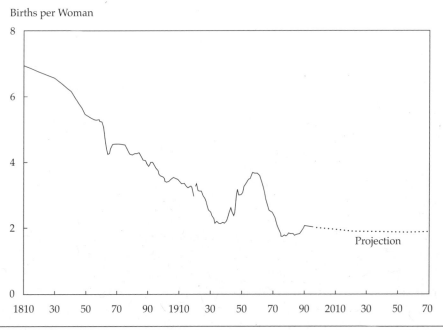

Sources: Data prior to 1920, Coale and Zelnick (1963); data from 1920 to 1969, Department of Health and Human Services; data from 1970 to 2070, Social Security Administration.

Figure 3.   Old-Age Dependency Ratio, 1900–2050

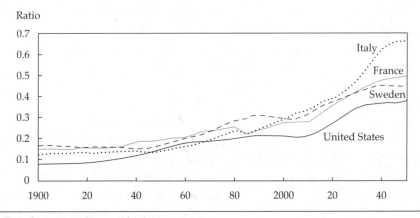

Note: Data for 2010–2050 are projections.
Sources: Based on data from the U.S. Census and the United Nations Population Information Network.

retire, with rough constancy projected afterwards. The old-age dependency ratio has become a standard term in the pension industry and is regularly and appropriately cited as part of the reason for the problems in many public pension systems.

Migration rates are also a component typically included in determining historical and projected demographic trends. Allowing more immigration is one way a country can boost its labor supply, and certainly, advanced countries can attract vast numbers of workers if they so choose. However, its impact on long-run pension financing is minimal because immigrants, like natives, eventually grow old, retire, and make claims on the pension system. With the importance of the impact of migration on many aspects of a country, migration is not a variable that should be adjusted just for pension financing.

In addition to people living longer, men are retiring earlier—a double whammy for pension systems. Labor force participation rates for men older than 65 have fallen steadily since the late 1800s, from a high in the United States of a little more than 75 percent in 1880 to just less than 25 percent in 1990. A closer look at the U.S. data shows that the labor force participation rates for men ages 18 to 85 have declined for all ages over the 110-year period from 1880 to 1990 but most dramatically for the older ages (50 and older). The lower participation rates are presumably a function of a powerful income effect—that is, higher pay and greater wealth achieved in part through the easier accumulation of wealth. In addition, laborers are enjoying shorter work days, shorter work weeks, shorter work years, and shorter working lives. Therefore, it is a mistake to think about the number of work years as a constant proportion of life expectancy because improvements in any number of areas, such as technical progress and productivity, are sure to chip away at that relationship.

The labor force participation rates for women, particularly younger women, tell a different tale. **Figure 4** compares the labor force participation rates of U.S. men and women for the 1950–2006 period according to two age groups—ages 55 to 64 and older than 65. Participation rates for the younger group of women steadily increased over the second half of the 20th century, in contrast to the declining participation rates for men of the same age. Older women, in contrast, maintained a relatively flat participation rate, reflecting the competing forces of new career opportunities and the prevailing trend toward earlier retirement.

Figure 4 also shows that the trend to earlier retirement has stopped. For the last 20 years, older male labor force participation has actually been rising slightly. It is important to recognize that the decline in participation rates appears to have ended, but it is also important to recognize that the offsetting rise does not resemble a force that would preserve a constant proportion of working years to retirement years because of the continued increase in longevity.

Figure 4. Annual Labor Force Participation Rate by Age and Sex, 1950–2006

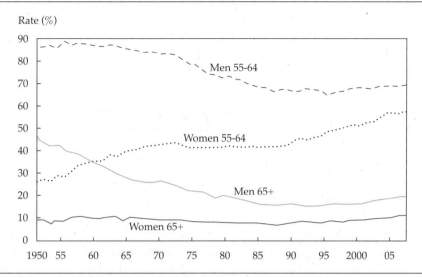

Source: Based on data from the Center for Retirement Research.

Pension Crisis Cause and Solutions

The pension crisis is essentially a failure to adapt to the long-term demographic trends of an increase in life expectancy, a decline in birth rate, and earlier retirement, even though the trends had been forecasted by the Office of the Chief Actuary of the U.S. Social Security Administration for many years. Superimposed on these trends is the increasing scale of pension systems since World War II and the baby boom. The latter two events are certainly aggravating factors in the pension crisis, but even in their absence, the pension crisis would have arisen.

Pension Reforms. Several countries, following various approaches, have attempted to adjust their overburdened public pension systems. I will review part of the reforms undertaken by four countries: Sweden, Germany, the United States, and the United Kingdom.

■ *Sweden.* In 1998, Sweden adopted a notional defined-contribution plan that is, in effect, a pay-as-you-go plan with the addition of a buffer stock of funding. The overall plan has a contribution rate of 18.5 percent, funded half by the employee and half by the employer. The majority of the contribution (16 percent) is credited to a notional account for the participant that grows over time from contributions and a notional return. The balance of the annual contribution (2.5 percent) goes to a fully funded individual account.

The Swedes call the partial funding of the notional accounts a "buffer stock" because it allows them to smooth the adjustment of the system, which is designed to mimic the adjustment of a defined-contribution plan. The plan administrator calculates participants' life expectancies and adjusts the benefits accordingly on a cohort-by-cohort basis. Participants are credited with accumulations as they work toward retirement. The accumulations are not based on actual rates earned by actual assets, however, but on a notional rate determined by a formula designed to keep a pay-as-you-go system sustainable. The plan administrator also has an override if the asset/liability mix gets out of line so that the notional rate can be adjusted. Such adjustment affects not just the accumulations of young workers toward their eventual retirement benefits but also the benefits that are in payout status. Therefore, when the economy is doing badly, the pension system can spread the risk among retirees and workers. This policy is consistent with finance theory—that risk should be spread very widely—although the extent of the spreading should vary with the degree of risk aversion of the risk taker.

Germany. The German pension system has been reformed repeatedly over recent years. Like the Swedish notional system, the German system is a pay-as-you-go plan. The Germans use a point system in which the participant earns points each year based on the relative amount of taxes paid on earnings. The points are then converted into pension benefits using a specified formula that includes an automatic adjustment for the old-age dependency ratio—in other words, for the ratio of the number of benefit recipients to the number of contributors (plus the unemployed).

United States. The U.S. pension system has three major components: defined-benefit plans, defined-contribution (savings) plans, and Social Security. Of these, only Social Security offers coverage to all. My comments focus on Social Security.

In 1983, the U.S. Congress raised the age of eligibility for receiving full Social Security retirement benefits from 65 to 67. For all born after 1959, the retirement age is 67. For those born in the years 1938 to 1959, the higher retirement age is gradually phased in based on the year of birth. In my opinion, rather than making further changes to the age for full benefits, a better approach is automatic indexing of benefit levels along the lines of the Swedish and German methods.

United Kingdom. The U.K. pension system has undergone a series of reforms in recent years. A key element has been to increase the state pension age and to encourage pensioners to delay receiving benefits with the carrot of receiving a larger benefit by waiting. The state pension age is now 65, but for pensioners who delay collecting benefits until age 66 or later, the benefits are more generous for each year of delay. That is, as the state pension age rises, the benefit at any age is lower because the pensioner is rewarded with a higher benefit for waiting to collect his or her pension for each year of delay beyond the new, higher pension age. For example, if a pensioner decides to retire, say, at 66 instead of 65 but at age 66 the state pension age has risen to 66, the pensioner will no longer get the anticipated increase in benefits for going a year past the state pension age. The increase from age 66 to 67, however, is unchanged.

Benefit Reductions vs. Revenue Increases. Sweden, Germany, the United States, and the United Kingdom have all adopted an approach that focuses on adapting to increasing pension expense by reducing benefits for any given retirement age, but of course, that is not the only way to adapt. Another possibility is to increase revenues. From the point of view of a public pension system, this solution means combining tax increases and benefit reductions. From the point of view of a plan participant, particularly one who does not wish to lengthen working years, this corresponds to the response of reducing spending, or consumption, both before and after retirement. The participant's per-year budget constraint is effectively reduced if the participant chooses not to increase the number of working years in proportion to total lifetime years.

Academics are not the only proponents of the two-pronged approach (raising taxes and reducing benefits) to solving the pension crisis. Blinder and Krueger (2004) conducted a survey in which they asked the public the best way to eliminate the Social Security deficit. The most frequent response, 34 percent, was for a combination of an increase in the payroll tax to fund the pension system and a reduction in benefits. Thirty percent of respondents wanted only to increase payroll taxes, and five percent wanted only to reduce benefits. Interestingly, roughly 22 percent proposed that neither option was necessary nor desirable, which is a puzzling and troubling response.

Let me reiterate that increasing the age at which a person can receive full pension benefits, as was done in the United States in 1983, is merely a device for cutting benefits and not a particularly good one at that. Let me illustrate. The benefit a participant gets if he or she retires at the age for full benefits is called the "primary insurance amount." Depending on when the participant begins to collect benefits, the primary insurance amount is multiplied by a certain percentage to calculate an adjusted benefit amount. Now suppose a worker currently has a full-benefit age of 67 (i.e., a benefit of 100 percent of the primary insurance amount is collected if the recipient retires at age 67). If the recipient retires earlier, the benefit is reduced, and if the recipient retires later, the benefit is increased. But if the age of full benefit for this worker is changed to 70, the 100 percent retirement benefit will not be paid until the participant reaches and starts benefits at age 70. If this worker still wants to start benefits at age 67, the benefit will be 80 percent of the primary insurance amount. The effect to the worker is a 20 percent benefit cut. But the words "benefit cut" never have to cross the lips of any politician when benefits are reduced in this way, which is probably what made it an attractive approach in 1983.

The sizes of the benefit cuts vary by the age at which the recipient begins to collect benefits. For an increase in the full-benefit age from 67 to 70, the size of the benefit cut is close to proportional for each age group, roughly 20 percent. But it is not exactly proportional, with workers retiring at age 62 suffering the largest benefit cut (only a little more than 20 percent at 21.4 percent). What do we know about people retiring at age 62? On average, they have the lowest lifetime earnings of all retired workers. They also have the shortest life expectancy of all retired workers. Can you imagine a politician standing up and saying, "I propose we cut benefits more for low earners with shorter lives than for high earners with longer lives"? Even though the percentage differences are small, I doubt that scenario would ever come to pass, but increasing the age for full benefits accomplishes the exact same thing without explicitly having to state the case.

Intergenerational Redistribution. An idea that is often tossed around as a solution to the pension crisis is increasing funding for public pensions. It is important to keep in mind that increasing funding for public pensions is a form of intergenerational redistribution. The idea is to raise taxes or cut benefits today so that in the future, taxes can be lower or benefits higher. That is an intergenerational redistribution. Is it a good idea or a bad idea? It depends on the nature of the trade-off between the changes today and the returns tomorrow, which is a function, first, of the return on assets and, second, of how well-off future generations will be compared with earlier generations.

Most important, however, is recognizing that increasing funding for public pensions sets up a trade-off of helping one group while hurting another. Regardless of any merits, it is not a painless cure. Some analysts have even argued that public funding of individual accounts is a third option—increasing taxes, reducing benefits, or creating individual accounts—for ameliorating the pension crisis. That idea is nonsense. Some analysts claim that because the rate of return on assets is expected to be higher than the growth rate of wage earnings, more funding is necessarily good. That argument looks sensible when considering only the long run but makes the mistake of ignoring current generations because current workers will receive fewer benefits or pay higher taxes to make it possible for future generations to receive greater benefits or pay lower taxes. It is wrong to do policy analysis without considering the full pattern of impacts.

Four Solutions. Four main courses of action are typically suggested as solutions to the pension crisis: higher contributions, lower monthly pensions, later retirement at the same full-benefit monthly pension (which is the U.K. solution), and policies designed to increase national output in order to afford a more generous pension system. Not included in this list is the option of increasing the earliest age when a participant can claim benefits, otherwise known as the state pension age in the United Kingdom and the earliest entitlement age in the United States.

By itself, increasing the earliest entitlement age for benefits would do nothing to ease the long-term financial position of the Social Security system. In the United States, the earliest entitlement age is 62. This demarcation has been part of the Social Security system for a long time, with no changes made to it in the 1983 reform amendments. But suppose the earliest age at which a participant can receive benefits is pushed back to age 63. At first, some savings will be realized when workers at age 62 do not make pension benefit claims and some continue to pay taxes into the system. But when age 63 rolls around for the workers who would otherwise have claimed benefits at age 62 but now are claiming at age 63, they will get a bigger benefit as a result of waiting and typically as a result of additional taxable earnings. The bigger benefit is approximately actuarially fair, which means that the system will pay the workers who begin receiving benefits at age 63—because of the higher benefits they will be paid over the rest of their lives—roughly enough to make up for the amount they were not paid at age 62. Therefore, later retirement is a boost to long-run finances only if it is accompanied by a reduction in the monthly pension bundled with it.

The Mix of Private and Public Pensions

The demographic trends affecting the pension industry do not clearly point to altering the mix of private and public pensions. A look at two of the trends shows why no obvious solution exists. First, the United States, the United Kingdom, and some other countries have experienced a much higher life expectancy growth rate for high earners than for low earners. One way to measure this phenomenon is by education, as illustrated in **Figure 5**, which shows the gap between the life expectancy of the top and bottom deciles of educational attainment for both white men and women. The gap grew dramatically over the 37 years from 1960 to 1997. Given the gap in life expectancy between low- and high-income earners, and given the importance of annuitization, public pensions with their progressive benefit formulas and benefit guarantees have been far more responsive to the needs of low-income earners than have private pensions. Indeed, the private pension system in the United States is disproportionately supportive of higher earners. Coverage rates and benefit levels in private plans are much better for high than for low earners.

A second trend that has potential implications for a solution that combines private and public pensions is the increasing variability in realized lifetime length and retirement age. Each of these factors makes a case for both a larger and a smaller reliance on public pensions. On the one hand, public pensions are designed to protect the most vulnerable groups in the community in a way that private pensions are not. On the other hand, private pension systems offer a degree of flexibility that is not present in public pensions. The public pension system allows workers the freedom to choose their retirement age, but everyone who is part of the system has the same payroll tax rate (up to an income cap, currently just more than $100,000 a year in the United States, above which taxes are not levied). In the private pension

Figure 5.   Decrease in U.S. Mortality Rate from Least to Most Educated

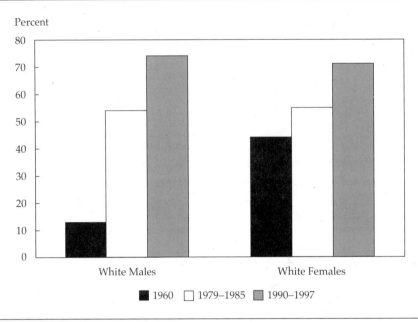

Source: Based on Elo and Smith (2003).

world, some systems are designed to meet the needs of earlier retirement of specific populations, such as police and firefighters and professional football players, whose jobs call for retirement much sooner than the norm. Adding this type of flexibility into a public pension system would be hard to design and implement.

The Social Security System

The Social Security system is extraordinarily important for the well-being of the elderly in the United States. A large portion of the elderly relies on Social Security for all or most of their income. In 2006, 64 percent of beneficiaries (52 percent of married couples and 72 percent of single individuals) depended on Social Security for half or more of their income and 32 percent of beneficiaries (20 percent of married couples and 41 percent of single individuals) depended on Social Security to supply 90 percent or more of their annual income. With the average benefits for an individual retired worker equal to roughly $1,000 a month, the heavy reliance on this income signifies its importance. Unmarried beneficiaries—mainly elderly widows and, to a lesser extent, elderly divorced women—are particularly reliant on their Social Security income. The data show that unmarried women have a very high poverty rate. Data for 2006 indicate that 16.8 percent of unmarried women are classified as poor and 10.2 percent are classified as near poor, more than three times the percentages of married elderly couples.

The disproportionate level of poverty in the elderly population (defined as the percentage of elderly receiving less than half the median income) is of particular concern in the United States at 20 percent and 30 percent for persons aged 66–74 and those aged 75 and over, respectively. Such rates are not unique to the United States; Japan and Australia share similar rates of poverty among their elderly populations, at 20 percent (Japan) and 21 percent (Australia) for ages 66–74 and 24 percent (Japan) and 29 percent (Australia) for ages 75 and older. In contrast, the poverty rate in the Netherlands for each of these two age groups is 2 percent, and in Canada, it is 4 percent and 5 percent, respectively. Both countries have noncontributory pensions for those over 65. In many countries, public pension systems are crucial to the survival of the elderly population.

Trends in Private Pensions

Over the 24 years from 1980 to 2004, an enormous shift from a private pension system dominated by defined-benefit (DB) plans to one dominated by defined-contribution (DC) plans occurred. **Figure 6** illustrates this dramatic about-face in terms of assets, benefits, active participants, and contributions, although the level of contributions had stabilized by 2004. This dramatic redistribution of assets from DB plans to DC plans is not just a U.S. phenomenon; the U.K. private pension system has experienced a similar change. In addition to this shift, many countries are following the lead of Chile and are moving toward funded individual accounts.

Figure 6. DC Plans as a Percentage of Total Plans: 1980, 1992, and 2004

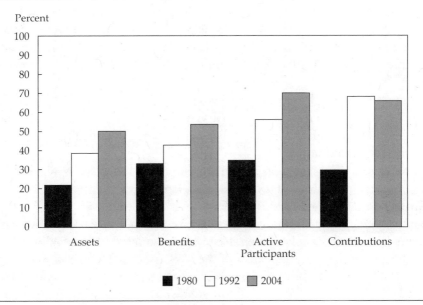

Source: Based on data from the Center for Retirement Research.

The recent huge decline in equity values may affect the trend toward DC plans, but I doubt it. With a $7.4 trillion decline in pension and household equity values from October 2007 to October 2008, workers are obviously suddenly aware that stocks, in general, and DC plans and IRAs, in particular, are a lot riskier than they thought before the downturn. At the same time, companies are also realizing that DB plans are much riskier than they thought before. These countervailing forces will likely act to maintain the current division between DC and DB plans, and the recent trend will not be reversed.

Many analysts, particularly politically liberal analysts, express great unhappiness at the broad move toward DC plans and away from DB plans, a view I do not share. I do have concerns that pension levels often drop relative to expectations when a company changes from a DB to a DC plan and that midcareer workers are suddenly subject to a different pension system, but as a general matter, I believe private DC plans are more advantageous for workers than are private DB plans and are easier to improve. Public systems, however, are a different matter. DB plans in public systems are very advantageous to participants. A prime advantage is their ability to share risk across successive generations. DC plans, however, are subject to market fluctuations that immediately affect the participants who have assets in the plan. DB plans, in contrast, can spread a negative market impact over a long time horizon.

Challenges.   Corporate DB pension plans have two problems. One is that they need to be well funded. Corporations can go out of business; even whole industries can shrink dramatically. The ability to actually pay the pension plan's obligations requires funding, unlike the federal government's ability to pay pension obligations through taxes and, if nothing else, printing money. Funding of a DB plan requires that when markets drop, to preserve adequate funding levels, the corporation has to increase its contribution levels. But it is precisely in times of a slowing economy, or a recession, that companies are in particular need of their cash and resist putting it into their pension plan. Therefore, the timing associated with required adjustments to DB plans is at odds with the ongoing business needs of the corporation. This inherent conflict compounds the difficulties surrounding corporate DB plan funding.

The second challenge associated with corporate DB plans is related to the poorly understood nature of the risks associated with them. If a plan is not adequately funded, then risk is shifted either to workers or to a third-party guarantor, which in the United States is the Pension Benefit Guaranty Corporation. Workers covered by a plan often have only a limited understanding of the risk–return frontier and of the nature of the risks associated with both equities and bonds, which creates problems for a worker's evaluation of the funding of DB plans as well as the working of DC plans. More subtle risks associated with DB pensions involve the value of the pension if the worker leaves employment, voluntarily or involuntarily; the chance that the company might change the terms of the pension plan, reducing expected benefits; and the impact of the company going out of business. Such risks are hard for most workers to understand. The reality is that DB pension plans are appealing only if they are perceived as pretty much fully guaranteed, which they are not, and if the scale of labor mobility is underplayed. Of course, public pension systems are not truly guaranteed either because adjustments have to be made to fine-tune the asset/liability mix. The adjustment process, however, encompasses a risk of a different sort, of a somewhat less onerous nature.

Other factors, or trends, that I have observed of late have informed my opinion that private DC plans are preferable for workers. As noted, the ability of DB plans to fulfill the needs of workers is harmed when workers are mobile, and workers are more mobile now than in the past. For example, in 2006, 46 percent of full-time employed men aged 58 to 62 were still employed by the same employer they worked for at age 50; earlier, in 1983, the number was 70 percent.

Progress. Several steps can be taken to improve the ability of pension systems to better meet the needs of workers and to lower their risks. First, workers must be better educated about the risks inherent in the design of their pension plans and how those risks may ultimately affect their retirement benefits. For DC plans, workers must learn how to construct sensible portfolios. In this regard they can be helped by a better array of options and well-chosen defaults. The second challenge is getting the government to pass sensible legislation about the risks associated with pension plans. For DB plans, the United States does not currently have a well-designed pension benefit guaranty program. And for DC plans, despite the Enron collapse, the United States has failed to enact the very sensible restriction on the amount of an employer's stock that can be held in the employees' pension plan. The result is that this type of pension risk remains widespread.

A second area in which progress can be made is seeking alternative approaches to the accumulate-assets-and-wait-until-retirement approach, which exposes the participant not only to fluctuations over the period in the investment portfolio but also to the pricing of annuities. An alternative is rolling annuitization. With rolling annuitization, workers are encouraged to buy annuities for their retirement throughout their working years to diversify the risk of annuity pricing and to take advantage of favorable markets for annuities rather than wait until retirement and be hostage to whatever the market for annuities is at that time. Rolling annuitization on an individual basis would be expensive, but if provided by the government through a group-type arrangement, it would be a manageable cost and an option worth thinking about.

IRAs, which are already a part of our retirement planning landscape, present a wonderful research opportunity. Several fascinating research questions wait to be answered, and among them is the question of how they should be taxed. In the

United States, standard IRAs are taxed at the point of distribution and Roth IRAs are taxed when funded. The two different structures came about for reasons driven more by politics than by an underlying analysis of the most sensible structure. It may well be advantageous to have both types of IRA exist, but a conclusion must await more research.

IRAs are an important part of the behavioral economics aspect of encouraging people to save for retirement. The question remains, however, about the best way to tax IRAs. Sweden has historically taxed part of the accumulation in these types of plans, and Australia did also for a while. Despite arguments that governments should not be taxing capital income at all, I believe doing so is part of an optimal tax plan. Having special tax treatment for assets that are set aside and held for a long time may represent more effective taxation of capital income because it avoids a long period of compounding of repeated taxation of capital income. Not much work has been done in this area, but I suspect it will be forthcoming.

Pension research needs to consider studies that integrate—from a behavioral point of view and a tax point of view—mandatory retirement savings and tax-favored retirement savings organized by corporations and by individuals. And because annuitization and accumulation affect the estates of individuals, the estate tax is an element that should be considered in addition to the annual income tax.

Conclusion

Finding a workable solution to the global pension crisis is important to the continued viability of pension systems and to the standard of living of both the workers who support the system and the retirees who are dependent on it. We can no longer afford to ignore the demographic trends that have caused our pension and retirement systems to become overburdened. The answer lies not only in reducing benefits, preferably with automatic adjustment to life expectancy, but also in increasing revenues to the system, which can respond to the same index as do benefits. Innovative alternatives to the status quo, such as rolling annuitization, should be considered in the beneficial interests of both current and future generations.

REFERENCES

Blinder, Alan S., and Alan B. Krueger. 2004. "What Does the Public Know about Economic Policy, and How Does It Know It?" NBER Working Paper 10787 (September).

Coale, A., and M. Zelnick. 1963. *New Estimates of Fertility and Population in the U.S.* Princeton, NJ: Princeton University Press.

Elo, Irma, and Kirsten P. Smith. 2003. "Trends in Educational Differentials in Mortality in the United States." Paper presented at the annual meeting of the Population Association of America, Minneapolis (May).

Question and Answer Session
Peter Diamond

Question: Is now the time for the Social Security system to begin investing in the stock market?

Diamond: Yes, I believe broadening the Social Security system's mandate to include stocks would be a very good move. Peter Orszag and I clearly stated in our book *Saving Social Security: A Balanced Approach* that we are in favor of having the Social Security Trust Fund diversify its portfolio and buy stocks. I also believe that, as part of a central bank's efforts to stabilize its economy, open market operations involving the buying and selling of stocks and bonds is a very sensible part of a central bank's toolkit. For example, Hong Kong bought into the Hong Kong stock market to prop it up when the market went into a serious decline and made quite a sizable profit when the market recovered. So, yes, I think the timing is great if the U.S. government were to get involved in the U.S. stock market now.

Question: But doesn't adding stock to the Social Security portfolio really amount to a tax on the owners of the equity risk premium?

Diamond: Not necessarily. A large fraction of Americans don't reap any gain from the equity premium because they have no equity exposure. In my view, the goal of diversifying the Social Security portfolio is that it will give people who otherwise wouldn't have access to it access to some of the market's return, and this would be advantageous to them. In addition, spreading the risk more widely in the economy will reduce the equity premium because, unlike a tax, spreading the risk is an improvement in efficiency, not a distortion in allocation. And getting more people involved in the stock market, even if the government is doing it on their behalf, would encourage more people to learn about the market, and the decline in the equity premium that's likely to follow from increased familiarity is a good thing, not a bad thing.

Question: In the current recessionary environment, we are certain to see impassioned pleas for reducing required contributions to DB plans. Is a reduction justifiable when newly contributed funds will go into the capital markets, where they will be invested and thus improve prospects for long-term employment?

Diamond: The determination of whether contributions should be made is a function of several variables, and primary among them is liquidity. Although some companies have retained earnings with which to fund contributions, others would have to borrow to make contributions and pay a significant liquidity premium to do so. The problem is that the substantial liquidity premium we are currently seeing in the market may impede the efficient allocations of investment resources. Another consideration is how the funds used to make the contributions would be used if the contributions were not made. The same consideration also applies to contributions to individual accounts. Is there a more efficient allocation in a recessionary economy than saving? Those judgments are hard to make. Capital markets aren't perfect, but they work well. The timing question is an interesting one and makes an insightful point.

Question: DB plans in the private sector have two advantages over DC plans: less expensive annuitization and more efficient allocation of capital. Is there any other way to get those advantages to individuals?

Diamond: It is possible to have group-provided annuities in a DC plan, although, in practice, companies that have moved to DC plans have frequently not provided annuity options to plan participants. I believe that is a mistake from a societal point of view, and I would not be at all troubled if DC plans were required to incorporate some DB plan options, such as annuitization. DB plans are increasingly allowing participants to take out a lump sum rather than take the defined benefits monthly, and adding a group annuity provision to a DC plan would not look all that different. As to the second point, I'm somewhat skeptical about the amount of social gain associated with DB plan management. For example, a plan that holds shares of its own company is not a good way to allocate resources. I think we are probably better off with well-directed DC plans. The important point is that plan participants must be given sensible investment guidance to place them at the appropriate place on the risk–return frontier. And recall that the literature comparing index funds with actively managed funds suggests that, by and large, actively managed funds are not adding to the value of the system given their additional administrative costs; this conclusion can inform the choice of investments for either DB or DC plans.

The Market for Long-Term Care

Amy Finkelstein

Professor of Economics, Massachusetts Institute of Technology
Co-Director, Public Economics Program, and Research Associate,
  National Bureau of Economic Research
Cambridge, Massachusetts

The need for long-term-care insurance is great, but the private market is small and is plagued by both demand-side and supply-side problems. Furthermore, it will be difficult to stimulate demand for private insurance given the crowd-out effect of Medicaid. One solution is to restructure Medicaid, but doing so could make the "cure" worse than the "disease."

For the past several years, I have been conducting research with Jeffrey Brown, who is at the University of Illinois at Urbana-Champaign and also at the National Bureau of Economic Research, to try to understand why the market for long-term-care insurance is so small and what would be the likely impact of alternative public policies on this market. In this presentation, I will give an overview of some of our findings.[1]

Research Motivation

Long-term care is one of the largest uninsured financial risks facing the elderly in the United States today. It is about 8½ percent of all health care spending for all ages and more than 1 percent of GDP. Moreover, long-term-care expenditures are predicted to triple in real terms by 2040, mostly because of increasing expected medical costs combined with the aging of the population. Another important and striking fact is the substantial variation across individuals in their long-term-care expenditures.

Two-thirds of 65-year-olds, for example, will never enter a nursing home. But for those who do, the burden is significant. For women who enter a nursing home, for example, one-quarter will be there more than three years—at more than $50,000 a year in expenditures, on average. So, long-term care is both a large and a variable expenditure. This is just the sort of risk where one would think that insurance would be extremely valuable. But most of this risk is not insured.

There is very little private insurance; only about 10 percent of the elderly have any private insurance. And this private insurance is quite limited in what it covers so that only about 4 percent of long-term-care expenditures are paid for by private insurance. By comparison, about 35 percent of all health care expenditures are paid for by private insurance.

---

[1]This research may be found at http://econ-www.mit.edu/faculty/afink.

Public insurance is also quite limited. Medicare, which is the principal public health insurance program for the elderly, really only covers acute care, and it does not cover long-term care. Medicaid, which is public health insurance for the poor, will cover long-term care in a nursing home but only as the payer of last resort; thus, it has stringent asset and income limitations. As a result, about a third of long-term-care expenditures are paid for out of pocket, which is double the fraction of expenditures paid out of pocket for the health sector as a whole.

The limited extent of insurance coverage for long-term care has important implications for the well-being of the elderly and, potentially, their adult children. These welfare implications will presumably become even more pronounced as the Baby Boomers age and as medical costs continue to rise.

Moreover, the limited size and efficiency of the private insurance market has implications for future government expenditures. A fact that is not often recognized is that currently a third of Medicaid expenditures are for long-term care. With Baby Boomers aging and costs going up, increasing pressure will be put on state and federal budgets. So, it is important to understand why people do not buy private long-term-care insurance and what can be done to stimulate this market.

The Long-Term-Care Market

About 10 percent of the elderly buy private long-term-care insurance. Men and women buy it in roughly even proportions. If your spouse has it, it is more likely that you will buy it, but often, people will insure just one spouse. Not surprisingly, but quite strikingly, the probability of owning long-term-care insurance is highly correlated with wealth. In the bottom quartile of the wealth distribution, only about 3 percent of the elderly report having long-term-care insurance. In the top wealth quartile, though, 19 percent report having long-term-care insurance. So, long-term-care insurance ownership is highly skewed by wealth.

Market Size Theories. There is an extensive theoretical literature on why this market is so small that looks at both the supply and the demand sides. On the demand side are theories about limited consumer rationality and crowd out. In terms of limiting consumer rationality, needing long-term care is an unpleasant event; people may not want to think about it. And in some cases, it is a small probability event, which people may have a hard time with. In addition, some researchers are concerned that people may not understand what, in fact, public insurance does and does not cover. People may think that Medicare covers more than it does or that Medicaid is easier to qualify for than it is.

The other main possibility on the demand side is factors that crowd out private insurance demand. One potential source of crowd out is Medicaid; it may crowd out private insurance demand because it does provide insurance (to those who qualify). Another potential source of crowd out is one's family; they may crowd out demand for formal private insurance by providing informal insurance; that is, the family may pay for care if it is needed or may provide in-kind, unpaid care.

There is also a range of possible supply-side factors that constrain the size of the private market. High transaction costs, imperfect competition, issues of asymmetric information—these are the standard litany of potential problems that can arise in insurance markets. One potential problem that is specific to this type of risk is the uninsured aggregate risk of rising long-term-care costs, which are hard to diversify cross-sectionally through traditional insurance means. There is also counterparty risk—the risk that the insurance provider will be insolvent or out of business, say, 30 years after the policy is purchased. Although this risk is mitigated by regulation of insurance company investment practices, the events of 2007–2009 suggest that no financial intermediary is completely safe.

Evidence of Supply-Side Problems. The typical policies that are purchased provide very limited benefits and do so at high prices. Consider the fact that the typical policy purchased covers only about a third of an individual's expected present discounted value of long-term-care expenditures. These policies usually have a $100 constant nominal daily benefit cap, which means whatever the nursing home expenditures are, the policy will reimburse only the first $100 of them (per day). Right now, the average daily cost of a nursing home is about $150 nationwide, and a lot of that benefit will be inflated away by the time it is needed. These policies, therefore, leave a significant share of expenditure risk uncovered.

The loads on these policies are also nontrivial. One can think about these loads in two different ways, and each gives different answers. For someone who buys a policy at age 65 and holds it until death, making premium payments every year, the typical load is about 18 cents on the dollar. So, for every dollar paid in premiums, the policyholder gets back about 82 cents in benefits. Premiums, moreover, are unisex; men and women face the same premiums (by law). But utilization is obviously much higher for women than for men. Thus, the actual loads are much higher for men than for women. These loads are about, on average, 45 cents on the dollar for men and about –5 cents on the dollar for women.

The load, however, is a lot larger if one takes into account the fact that most people do not continue making their premiums every year (about 7 percent of policies lapse each year). So, accounting for policy lapses raises the load to 51 cents on the dollar (i.e., about 49 cents in benefits). These loads are very high compared with traditional load estimates from other markets: 15–25 cents for annuities, 6–10 cents for group health insurance, and 25–40 cents for nongroup health insurance.

Role of Medicaid

I am sure these market problems—high prices and limited benefits—contribute to limited demand for private insurance. Indeed, it seems quite obvious that if prices were reduced, demand would increase. The question is, how much would it increase? One of our key findings is that even if all these market problems were corrected, very few people would buy long-term-care insurance given the existence of Medicaid. That is, even if policies were available that are both actuarially fair and comprehensive in terms of their coverage—which, as I have said, they currently are not—we estimate that at least two-thirds of the wealth distribution would still not buy insurance given the existence of Medicaid. This large crowd-out effect is happening despite the fact that Medicaid is a relatively poor insurance product for all but the poorest of individuals because of its stringent income and asset tests.

This large crowd-out effect of Medicaid comes from the fact that Medicaid imposes a large *implicit tax* on private policies. In other words, much of the premium for private policies is going to pay for benefits that, if the individual had not bought that policy, Medicaid would have paid for. For median wealth individuals, we estimate that 60–75 percent of the benefits they are getting from a private policy duplicate benefits that Medicaid would otherwise have paid. The loads referred to earlier are gross loads from the insurance company perspective; they are the percentage of premiums paid in that are not paid out as benefits. But from the individual's perspective, the net load—where benefits received are adjusted by subtracting what that person would have received from Medicaid had he or she not bought this policy—is very high.

This large implicit tax comes from two features. First, Medicaid is a secondary payer. That is, if the individual is eligible for Medicaid (meets the income and asset requirements) but has a private policy, the private policy pays first. Medicaid then pays for benefits not covered by the private policy. The second factor is that Medicaid is means tested: You have to have relatively limited income and assets to receive Medicaid. One of the major functions of private insurance is to protect your assets, but in doing so, it reduces the probability that you receive any benefit from Medicaid. So, absent the private insurance, you would have to spend down a lot of your assets, which obviously has negative implications, but then Medicaid would end up paying for a lot of your long-term care.

We have found that eliminating one but not the other—that is, either making Medicaid a primary payer but leaving the asset test or leaving Medicaid as a secondary payer but eliminating the asset test—is not enough to substantially reduce this implicit tax. But restructuring Medicaid to reduce the implicit tax is a hard problem, and I do not have a good solution. I know of two solutions, neither of which appeals to many people. One extreme solution is to include long-term-care coverage in Medicare, making it universal and not means tested. It would then crowd out all private insurance, but at least it would be providing relatively comprehensive coverage.

The second solution is to try to design a policy that eliminates the Medicaid implicit tax. For example, if you purchased a private long-term-care insurance policy that is comprehensive, you could get a refundable tax credit equal to the expected present discounted value of the Medicaid costs. Basically, because you are buying private insurance, you will not have as many Medicaid expenditures, so you can get a refundable tax credit. Conceptually, that solution is relatively straightforward. In practice, it is virtually impossible to implement. The expected present discounted value of Medicaid and, therefore, how much the tax credit should be will vary with your wealth and with your health. Wealthier people will get less back from Medicaid, as will healthier people. But wealth and health are difficult for the government to observe accurately. So, providing a generalized tax credit for buying a private insurance policy would likely create extreme adverse selection problems.

Although I thus do not have a good solution to the problems created by the Medicaid implicit tax, I would like to raise it as a challenge and an important area for further work.

Conclusion

Jeffrey Brown and I have found notable supply-side market imperfections in the long-term-care market, but they do not seem to be the primary cause of the limited market size in the sense that just eliminating these private market failures is unlikely to stimulate much demand for private insurance. On the demand side, we are finding that the public Medicaid program severely constrains demand for private insurance, even though Medicaid itself is not good insurance except for the very poor. Of course, this does not mean that Medicaid reform that eliminates (or substantially reduces) the Medicaid implicit tax would be *sufficient* to stimulate the private market (because, as I have noted, supply-side problems also exist). Our research, however, does suggest that such reform is *necessary* for substantially increasing the size of the private long-term-care insurance market.

Question and Answer Session

Amy Finkelstein

Question: What's happened to the public/private partnership programs that have been established in the last 10 or 15 years?

Finkelstein: In four states that I know of—California, New York, Indiana, and Connecticut—these programs are still running. But they are not active because very few people actually end up participating in them.

Although each of the programs is slightly different, the basic idea is that in return for buying private insurance, the state relaxes the means-testing threshold for Medicaid or for state public assistance. So, if you've bought private insurance, you don't have to spend down as much before Medicaid will come in. The problem is that Medicaid is still a secondary payer; thus, part of what your private insurance has now paid for is benefits that, absent private insurance, Medicaid would have ultimately paid for.

So, our estimates at least were consistent with the fact that people didn't seem to be buying these policies.

Question: Is mandatory coverage a solution?

Finkelstein: Mandatory insurance coverage is one important and natural solution to a large problem of the uninsured. That's certainly one way to address the fact that what you currently have is a public insurance program that's crowding out private insurance demand without providing comprehensive coverage.

Mandatory public insurance, of course, has its own issues. Does everyone want the same insurance policy? Probably not. But then you get into possibly mandating a bare-bones policy and allowing people to upgrade. There's some reason to be concerned that you might get more adverse selection problems on that residual upgrading market than on the overall market.

Health, Wealth, and Retirement

Jonathan Skinner
John Sloan Dickey Third Century Professor of Economics
Dartmouth College and Dartmouth Institute for
    Health Policy and Clinical Practice
Hanover, New Hampshire

Some researchers say Americans are not saving enough for retirement, and some say not to worry; retirement savings are just fine. Both groups may be right but for different stages in the retirement cycle. The trend with out-of-pocket medical expenses, however, could tip that balance.

The information on retirement preparedness can be quite confusing. Some research shows that half of all Americans are not prepared for retirement, but then other studies indicate that people are saving just fine for retirement (i.e., don't worry). In this presentation, I will muddy the waters even further and talk about out-of-pocket health care expenses and how they fit in with retirement planning.[1]

New View: Don't Worry

The new view on retirement savings seems to be "Don't worry so much." Aguiar and Hurst (2005) have found that in retirement, household production substitutes leisure for consumption. In other words, when you retire, you have a lot of time. You do not need to go out to eat and spend money; rather, you have the time to stay home and make a wonderful pasta sauce and save money. Another explanation why you do not need as much for retirement is that you have been endlessly chasing dollars all your life and now you have time to step back and think about what is really important (see Eisenberg 2006 and Brock 2004). Maybe you should sit down and write the great American novel or go and volunteer in an elderly day care center; if that is all you need, you do not need much money to do that.

But people do not always consider that it is possible to live as many years retired as not retired—or more. It is not unheard of for someone to work from age 25 to 62 and then live to 105. Retirement should thus be thought of in very, very different stages of the life cycle. In early retirement, people can substitute. They can get by on not much. They can travel off-season and buy inexpensive groceries because they have the time to shop around a little more. In other words, they can (to some extent) substitute leisure for expenditures.

---

[1]This presentation is based on Skinner (2007).

But there is the later stage that concerns me much more when you can no longer do that. In fact, your productivity has declined a lot. Medical care is especially difficult to produce yourself. So, you have to come up with the money (which can be hard) or rely on the government safety net—Medicaid.

The Role of Medicaid

In standard economic models, Medicaid benefits are usually assumed to be the same quality as those that come from spending your own money. But some interesting research is coming from Vincent Mor's group at Brown University about differences in the quality of nursing homes (see Mor, Zinn, Angelelli, Teno, and Miller 2004). They have developed a dataset on the quality of nursing homes by surveying them about deficiencies (such as bed sores) in the quality of care they are providing. Such quality concerns are extremely important if you have a parent at a nursing home or if you are a patient yourself. What they have found is that so-called bottom-tier nursing homes are almost entirely paid for by Medicaid, as shown in **Table 1**. Furthermore, note that in the bottom tier, the number of registered nurse full-time equivalents (FTEs) is 3.4 per 100 residents, compared with 5.5 in the top tier.

Table 1. "Top-Tier" vs. "Bottom-Tier" Nursing Homes

Measure	Top Tier	Bottom Tier
Percentage of nursing homes	87%	13%
Registered nurse FTEs per 100 residents	5.5	3.4
Percentage psychiatric diagnosis	11.5%	22.3%
Quality deficiencies	7.9	12.3

Notes: This table distinguishes between what Mor et al. (2004) designate as top-tier and bottom-tier nursing homes. Residents of the lower-tier nursing homes are largely Medicaid patients. These lower-tier nursing homes also exhibit a higher fraction of patients with psychiatric diagnoses and quality deficiencies.

Source: Based on data from Mor et al. (2004).

All of these measures point to worse care in the bottom-tier, primarily Medicaid, facilities. Medicaid is certainly an option, but it is not the greatest option. More research needs to be done about the vast variation in the quality of care across nursing homes and how savings can at least get you into a higher-quality nursing home, even if ultimately you end up on Medicaid. The key is having enough cash so that top-tier facilities will let you in.[2]

---

[2]It is a common practice, at least in the United States, for the better long-term-care facilities to accept a blended payment schedule consisting of the patient's own money at the beginning then the lower Medicaid reimbursement when the patient's own money runs out. Thus, it is to the patient's advantage to have his or her own funds (or access to family funds) even if those funds will eventually be spent down to the point where the patient goes on Medicaid.

Wealth Levels Near Death

Another issue I have been struck by is how much wealth seems to disappear near death. An article by French, De Nardi, Jones, Baker, and Doctor (2006) shows that wealth basically was cut in half in the last four years of life. Reported medical expenses actually account for only about a third of that loss. I have conducted some work with Kathleen McGarry, also at Dartmouth, that suggests a lot of this difference is underreporting. We suspect money is flowing out toward the end of life, but we cannot always find it in the survey data.

Figure 1 gives further evidence of this phenomenon. It shows out-of-pocket expenditures by wealth quartile near the end of life, and as can be seen, they are strongly related to wealth. Basically, in the last year or so of life, spending is $16,000 on average for the highest wealth quartile and only $8,000 for the lowest wealth quartile, which is a large difference. One might think that this difference comes from fancy nursing homes, but that seems unlikely. Nor does it have much to do with physician payments or even prescription drugs. Instead, it is about what people pay to be able to remain in their house and avoid going into a nursing home—including helpers.

Conclusion

In the first stage of retirement—when you are 65 or 70—it is not critical to have put aside a lot of money if you have an active lifestyle, if you are in good health, if you like doing things that do not cost much. But the problem is later on in life, in the second stage. Data from the U.S. Social Security Advisory Board suggest that out-of-pocket health care expenses in the future could consume as much as 70 percent of average Social Security benefits. Another study by Johnson and Penner (2004) suggests that much of the Baby Boomers' future earnings growth will be absorbed by out-of-pocket medical expenses, which are growing at an even faster rate.

Of course, these depressing predictions are all subject to uncertainty; they could be worse or better than expected. The problem is how to plan for uncertainty. My advice would be to save more, especially because many people have argued that Medicare and Social Security will go bust. But even if they do not go bust, I would rather reach retirement with more money than less. Housing wealth is particularly valuable, and it is often sheltered from Medicaid spend-down rules. Another possibility if you do not want to save so much is to "invest" in having a family and live near your children (although you should probably check with your children first). A further option is to save for low-cost contingencies. In other words, save for the $50,000 expense that can make your house livable for an extra six months before you have to go into a nursing home. And finally, despite the high administrative loads for long-term-care insurance, such insurance could still be a very good option to consider.

Figure 1.   Out-of-Pocket Expenditures by Wealth Quartile Near the End of Life

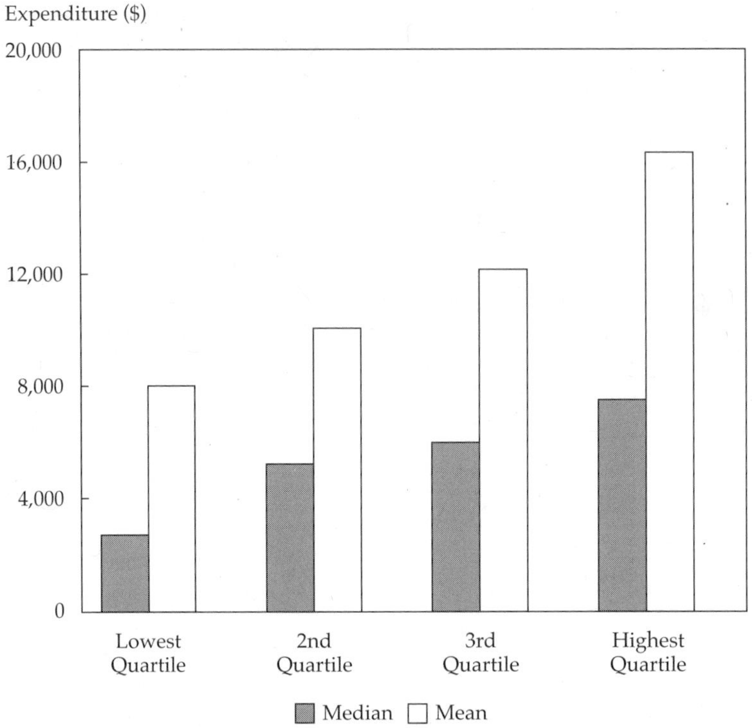

Expenditure ($)

[Bar chart showing expenditures by wealth quartile. The y-axis ranges from 0 to 20,000 in increments of 4,000. Four groups (Lowest Quartile, 2nd Quartile, 3rd Quartile, Highest Quartile) each show Median (shaded) and Mean (open) bars.]

- Lowest Quartile: Median ≈ 2,700; Mean ≈ 8,000
- 2nd Quartile: Median ≈ 5,300; Mean ≈ 10,000
- 3rd Quartile: Median ≈ 6,000; Mean ≈ 12,200
- Highest Quartile: Median ≈ 7,500; Mean ≈ 16,400

■ Median □ Mean

Source: Based on data from McGarry and Skinner (2008).

REFERENCES

Aguiar, Mark, and Erik Hurst. 2005. "Consumption versus Expenditure." *Journal of Political Economy*, vol. 113, no. 5 (October):919–948.

Brock, Fred. 2004. *Live Well on Less Than You Think*. New York: Henry Holt.

Eisenberg, Lee. 2006. *The Number: A Completely Different Way to Think About the Rest of Your Life*. New York: Free Press.

Fisher, E.S., M. McClellan, S. Lieberman, J. Bertko, J. Lee, J. Lewis, and J. Skinner. 2009. "Fostering Accountable Health Care: Moving Forward in Medicare." *Health Affairs*, vol. 28, no. 2 (March/April; web-exclusive content):w219–w231.

French, Eric, Mariacristina De Nardi, John Bailey Jones, Olesya Baker, and Phil Doctor. 2006. "Right before the End: Asset Decumulation at the End of Life." *Economic Perspectives*, Federal Reserve Bank of Chicago, vol. 30 (Third Quarter).

Johnson, Richard W., and Rudolph G. Penner. 2004. "Will Health Care Costs Erode Retirement Security?" Issue in Brief, Center for Retirement Research, Boston College (October).

McGarry, K., and J. Skinner. 2008. "Out-of-Pocket Medical Expenses and Retirement Security." NBER Working Paper NB07-03 (February).

Mor, V., J. Zinn, J. Angelelli, J.M. Teno, and S.C. Miller. 2004. "Driven to Tiers: Socioeconomic and Racial Disparities in the Quality of Nursing Home Care." *Milbank Quarterly*, vol. 82, no. 2:227–256.

Skinner, Jonathan. 2007. "Are You Sure You're Saving Enough for Retirement?" *Journal of Economic Perspectives*, vol. 21, no. 3 (Summer):59–80.

Question and Answer Session
Jonathan Skinner

Question: So, are people overprepared or underprepared for retirement?

Skinner: Some people think that there really isn't a retirement savings issue. I think there is, although not for everybody. Some people save a lot. When people have a lot of wealth and they have good pensions, their consumption actually tends to rise in retirement. But when people don't have very good pensions and they haven't saved much wealth, their consumption drops. That's not a behavioral issue; that's an implication of the budget constraint. Some estimate that 40 percent of people are unprepared. We've found that maybe 25 percent of people experience substantial drops in consumption near retirement. And rising health care costs, if anything, just make declines in consumption more of an issue, at least for an increasing (and I suspect substantial) fraction of the population.

Question: What does the future of Medicare look like?

Skinner: Jack Wennberg and Elliott Fisher have been looking at inefficiency in Medicare. Some hospitals and physician groups can deliver care at about half the cost of other, less-efficient providers. So, there's a tremendous amount of inefficiency, and we're now getting to the point where we can identify low-cost, high-quality hospitals and provider groups.

In collaboration with others, I've suggested at least one approach to reducing Medicare costs, but there are many other options that should be considered.[3]

---

[3] See Fisher, McClellan, Lieberman, Bertko, Lee, Lewis, and Skinner (2009).

The Case for Phased Retirement

Anna M. Rappaport
President
Anna Rappaport Consulting
Chicago

Phased retirement offers many older workers a positive work/life balance that allows them to lead less stressful lives and to remain productive—financially, socially, and intellectually—as they approach full-time retirement. Data show that highly skilled and educated employees are most likely to have the ability to phase. Some employers have adopted phased retirement programs or offered phased retirement informally, often rehiring retired employees.

The term "phased retirement" has been used to mean different things to different people. In this presentation, I focus on phased retirement as being any arrangement that allows people to move in stages from full-time work to not working.

Reasons for Phased Retirement

About 5 in 10 people work after retirement or phase out of the workforce in some way, and more than 7 in 10 people say they would like to work during their retirement years. These statistics indicate a shift in priorities. For many working people, being in career mode means that their job is their number one focus; that is, they plan their lives around their careers. Many workers may even feel that their employer seems to own them 24/7. But when people begin to think about retirement and approach retirement age, their mind-set changes and their life priorities shift. Although working into retirement is part of the picture, they want work to fit around their lifestyle rather than making their lifestyle fit around work.

Roughly 4 in 10 people retire earlier than they had anticipated, yet few people actually plan for premature retirement risk. People are forced into early retirement for a number of reasons, including job loss, illness, or the need to be a caregiver for a family member. In the 2007 Risks and Process of Retirement Survey conducted by the Society of Actuaries, a third of respondents claimed that retirement did not apply to them, which seems to be another way of saying that they did not plan to retire. Yet when I ask people who say they do not plan to retire if they expect to work after age 75, the typical answer is no. Therefore, a more accurate interpretation of their response may be that people just want to retire later than the age they perceive to be the norm. Interestingly, in several different studies, many more people indicated that they would like to work after retirement than actually do. Maintaining or obtaining the appropriate skills to work longer is a big problem in some occupations, and older applicants generally have more difficulty getting jobs. All of these factors, and others, combine to create a puzzle for many that is called "retirement"—with the larger pieces being the "when" and "how."

Phased retirement encompasses a range of definitions and work/lifestyle combinations, including arrangements that

- allow mature workers to work on a reduced or modified basis before retirement (phasing preretirement),
- allow retirees to be rehired (phasing postretirement),
- modify work through a change of schedule, place, or duties, and
- enable workers who are eligible for retirement to collect some portion of their pension benefits as they continue to work.

The phased retirement arrangement can be formal or informal and can involve working for a former employer or a new employer. It may include any or several of the features described here. As a consequence, there is no agreement among experts about the "right" definition.

The stakeholders who have an interest in phased retirement are the individuals facing retirement, employers, shareholders of the companies that retirees work for, and the public at large. Anyone who is 50 years old or older needs appropriate employment options for the future, which increasingly include some form of phased retirement. Employers and shareholders need talent and good results, both of which can be maintained by keeping experienced employees. And the public at large needs a well-functioning economy and, as consumers, good products and services. Thus, many parties stand to benefit from phased retirement options for retirees.

Gradual retirement, or phasing, falls onto a spectrum that can be thought of in terms of its end points—phasing a little and phasing a lot. Phasing a little means that the individual maintains a regular work schedule but with somewhat reduced hours. The phasing retiree is considered a regular employee with an ongoing commitment to his or her employer and continues to receive a predictable income and health benefits. The individual, however, is unlikely to receive pension payments. The result is that the individual acquires some modest flexibility in work/life balance, although the work options offered by the employer are similar to those offered to other employees; that is, there is minimal special treatment for individuals phasing a little.

Phasing a lot, however, means a lot of change. In the aggregate, phasing a lot includes a number of schedule options, such as being on call or part of a pool, seasonal work, or job sharing. It is up to individual retirees to work out an acceptable deal or search out the option of choice. Most retirees, except nurses and certain other health care professionals, have a limited range of options. Typically, the retiree operates as a temporary employee or consultant and does not enjoy a regular work commitment or salary from the employer, nor health benefits. Unlike someone who is phasing a little, someone who is phasing a lot *is* likely to receive pension benefits.

Phasing a lot often provides a great deal of personal flexibility and typically a set of different work options. Specific options available to an individual depend on negotiations and what arrangements can be found (see **Exhibit 1** for a comparison of phasing a little and phasing a lot).

Exhibit 1. Different Options for Phased Retirement

Item	Phasing a Little	Phasing a Lot
Schedule options	For example: • Working 20% fewer hours or compressing work into fewer days • Taking extra vacation time • Commitment to work at least 70% of usual schedule on flexible basis—design option to fit	For example: • 60% or less of usual work hours or workload • Seasonal or occasional work • On-call status • Project work • Job sharing
Employment relationship	A regular employee	May be viewed as a regular employee, a temp, or a consultant
Pension payments likely to be part of the arrangement	Usually not, at present. It remains to be seen whether partial payments after age 62 will become more common under the new law	Yes, particularly for those people who are working in retirement
Level of commitment and job definition required	Ongoing commitment to specific job and job definition	May involve ongoing commitment or may allow choosing whether to work on a project-by-project basis
Gain in flexibility for company and employee	Moderate	Can be very large
Income predictability	Same as for regular job	Limited predictability, except in high-demand occupations
Employer health benefits	Preretirement phasing most attractive if health benefits remain available	• Retiree health coverage is unaffected by phasing • Postretirement phasers are usually not entitled to receive same health benefits as active employees. Therefore, this option may not be feasible for those who lack retiree health benefits or coverage through another family member and/or who are not yet Medicare-eligible
Flexible work options, such as different length shifts and part time	Often same flexible work options as those offered to other employees	Flexible work options may be different from those offered to other employees

Source: Based on data from "Phased Retirement after the Pension Protection Act," The Conference Board (2007).

The distinction between phasing pre- and postretirement can be explained by using the case of a bank teller. A bank teller who is phasing preretirement typically might work three or four days a week on a regular basis as a regular employee at a regular location. After reaching age 62, the teller might be paid a partial pension, but most employers do not do so. A bank teller who is phasing postretirement might have a regular assignment, or the individual might fill in for colleagues who are vacationing or on disability, or the person might be on call to fill in as needed and thus work at various bank branch locations. The teller would likely have a temporary status or be a member of a retiree pool and receive pension benefits as well as compensation for work performed (see **Exhibit 2** for more detail and for an added example—that of a research scientist).

Exhibit 2. Phased Retirement Options Applied to Different Jobs

Position	Phasing Preretirement	Phasing Postretirement
Bank teller	• Work four days a week on an ongoing basis • Work as a regular employee • Work at the "normal" work location • In the future, could be paid partial pension after age 62, if company policy allows	• Work as fill-in during vacations or on call during the year • Work as a temporary or through a retiree pool • In a bank with multiple branches, might be able to work in different locations, but working from home or from a seasonal residence not possible • Paid pension and appropriate compensation for work
Research scientist	• Move out of management role, take on mentoring of some younger scientists, and reduce number of projects • Paid salary on prorated or other agreed-upon basis, rather than by the job or project • Potential for a lot of flexibility of time with agreed-upon commitment; type of work being done may or may not require specific location • Could be paid partial pension if after age 62 in addition to salary; at present, unlikely that such payment is being made	• Serve as adviser, trainer, or team member on specific projects • Paid pension and part salary, or paid by hour or project while collecting pension • Time commitment as agreed upon; work probably involves significant flexibility of place

Source: Based on data from "Phased Retirement after the Pension Protection Act," The Conference Board (2007).

From the employee's perspective, phased retirement is a good transition from full-time work to full-time retirement for several reasons. A gradual transition can be more comfortable than a radical overnight change. And because of the stressful careers and 60-hour workweeks that so many people find themselves in today, they have added interest in phased retirement. People who would be happy to continue working 35 or 40 hours a week do not feel the same way about a 60-hour workweek. In addition, many people in their 50s and 60s have family members—in particular, older parents or spouses—who need care, which for people in full-time, demanding jobs can present an enormously stressful situation. I know a number people who have taken a leave of absence or left jobs in their 50s because of the challenges of aging parents.

Phased retirement offers people a means to meet their family responsibilities without having to totally give up their jobs. Disability and physical limitations also encourage people to think about phased retirement. And when both spouses work and one retires, often the other follows suit or prefers to work fewer hours so that the couple can spend more personal time together. Also, after working for many years, most people would prefer to spend their remaining working life on projects of their choosing during the hours of their choosing. Essentially, the quest is to find a work/life balance that fits the employee's needs as well as those of the employer after the employee has put the employer's needs first for many years.

From the employer's perspective, phased retirement also offers numerous advantages. A major advantage is that it helps retain company-specific human capital as well as the types of expertise that are difficult to find and replace. Another advantage is that when regular staff members do not have time for special projects, experienced employees participating in phased retirement programs may have the time and skills to undertake such tasks. It has become increasingly difficult to get special projects done today because staffs have been cut so deeply and almost everyone is overworked.

Former employees are also an ideal resource to help with training new employees. Managing peak workloads, including unpredictable peaks, is another reason employers support phased retirement. Flexibility and redundancy can also be gained by using phased retirees to staff round-the-clock customer service as well as to meet variable workloads and seasonal work patterns. Other reasons for employers to support phased retirement are the ability to keep promotion paths open and to have the resources to fill in for employees who become disabled or who take vacation.

Case Study

The Bon Secours Richmond Health System has been offering its employees phased retirement options for a number of years. In fact, its policy has been so progressive that it has been widely cited. Bon Secours offers a formal program that includes three methods for an employee to phase into retirement. First, the employee can retire at age 65 but continue working part time (up to 24 hours a week) and collect a full pension. Second, the employee can work past age 70½ and receive a pension check regardless of the schedule worked. Third, the employee can retire and then return after three months. That employee will continue to collect a pension and can work any schedule.

Retired employees who choose to work 1,000 hours a year continue to receive pension credit, and those who work more than 16 hours a week qualify to participate in health benefits, regardless of age. As of September 2008, 80 of the 170 employees who were older than age 65 were phasing. The Bon Secours workforce is 85 percent female, and most participants are very pleased with this program.

The Bon Secours experience also offers insight into what phased retirement means to individual employees. In a webcast sponsored by The Conference Board, Dawn Malone from Bon Secours Health System shared how some employees had made phased retirement work:

> In this next scenario, we'll look at Nettie's career. She began nursing in 1957. She worked on three units. She was one of the first "working mothers" to request flex scheduling to accommodate child care issues. Her husband was in the military and was gone for months at a time. She was originally hired to work 3 p.m. to 11 p.m. However, with small children at home and child-care issues interfering with her work schedule, Nettie lobbied the Nursing Director to allow her to flex her schedule. She worked 7 a.m. to 7 p.m. for many years.
>
> In 1975, she transferred to Employee Health. During this time, she also worked PRN evenings, and weekends on the units. This made her the first employee allowed to work in more than one cost center—another flex scheduling milestone. In 1999, she retired. Then in January 2000, she returned to work for Employee Wellness. Among other duties, she performs TB skin tests on employees. She has gradually reduced her hours since retirement. She currently works two days per week.[1]

Nettie and several other examples make phased retirement seem much more understandable and demonstrate how individuals apply skills in different roles.

Rehiring Retirees

The most common form of phased retirement is rehiring retirees, which can be done directly or using a third-party arrangement. Five companies offer examples of the success of such a strategy for both the employer and the employee. The first is the Southern Company, an electric utility headquartered in Atlanta. It has an in-house pool of rehired retirees who are available for tasks such as repairing downed power lines after emergencies (e.g., hurricanes) when resources beyond normal levels are required—an example of meeting peak loads caused by unpredictable events.

---

[1] Anna M. Rappaport, "Some Interesting Information about Phased Retirement," *Pension Section News*, the Society of Actuaries (January, 2008): http://newsletters.soa.org/soap/issues/2008-01-31/7.html.

The Aerospace Corporation has a retiree casual employment program composed of 600 participants, with about 300 working at any one time. These rehired retirees are able to continue to support the mission of their employer by applying their years of experience and unique, scientific skills in a flexible work format. Monsanto Company has established a Resource Re-Entry Center that is available to all former employees, including retirees, wishing to return to Monsanto in a temporary capacity. The MITRE Corporation—a not-for-profit organization with expertise in systems engineering, information technology, and enterprise modernization—has a program somewhat like the Aerospace Corporation's retiree casual employment program called Reserves at the Ready.

This next example is a third-party solution: YourEncore is a consulting and innovation company that as of July 2008 supported 30 of the Fortune 500 companies with a team of 4,000 scientific and engineering experts. Retirees are rehired by YourEncore on a project basis, and then YourEncore offers consulting services to its clients. Retirees may provide service to their former employer or another company, but they may not work more than 1,000 hours a year. YourEncore focuses on highly specialized work performed by experts.

All of these programs provide employers with the expertise they need when they need it and provide employees the opportunity to remain in the workforce in a way that is convenient for them.

Even though the rehiring of retirees has been shown to work well for all stakeholders, barriers exist to widespread adoption of these types of programs. One significant barrier is legal uncertainty, including confusion about what constitutes bona fide termination of employment as well as a lack of clarity regarding age discrimination issues. Independent contractor rules and suspension of benefits rules also muddy the waters. In addition to the legal barriers is the problem that finding ways to offer phased retirement is often not a high priority.

Some employers have addressed these barriers by rehiring retirees and by requiring that former employees wait three to six months before they are rehired. Some have set up internal temporary retiree pools or general temporary pools where retirees can participate. In addition, an employer may limit the working hours of rehires to less than 1,000 hours a year. Others use a third-party solution in which an outside firm hires former employees. And certainly, third-party solutions may be used in combination with other arrangements.

Who Is Phasing Now?

Experience shows that older workers with higher levels of education are more likely to work on a part-time basis (i.e., be a "phaser") than either to continue to work on a full-time basis or to move to full-time retirement. That is, among those who want to work, human capital can be a factor in who can find part-time employment or negotiate it with their employer. According to an analysis by Tay McNamara, who is at the Sloan Center on Aging & Work at Boston College, of the 2004 Health and Retirement Study (HRS) conducted by the University of Michigan, women, more-educated workers, and older workers are more likely to participate in a phased retirement program. Also, based on the responses of participants in this 2004 HRS, 12.3 percent were currently phasing into retirement; approximately two of every five (39.8 percent) of these phasers were working part time for their former full-time employer; and 44.9 percent of the phasers were working part time for a new employer.

Moreover, an analysis of the 2004 HRS data reveals that 47.6 percent of all retirees had phased into retirement, with 16.4 percent moving from full-time to part-time work for the same employer before accepting full-time retirement and 31.1 percent moving from full-time to part-time work (but not necessarily for the same employer).

Recommendations

I have several policy recommendations that are based on what I believe is a desirable and viable move toward phased retirement. First, public education is needed to inform future retirees about the implications of various retirement ages so that they better understand the impact on Social Security benefits, defined-contribution account balances, defined-benefit plan benefits, and retirement resources for various time periods.

Second, a multidisciplinary effort is needed to raise awareness about the benefits of rehiring retirees and utilizing this underused labor force by writing information papers on the subject that clarify the pertinent issues and discuss the topic from both the employee's and employer's perspectives. The papers should include the types of opportunities that may be available, the types of third parties that support "third age" (partly retired) individuals, and issues in negotiating for alternative work arrangements and contracting if the retiree will be working as a contractor, which involves a mix of human resource, legal, actuarial, and business issues. It is hoped that these information papers could come from a neutral, creditable source, such as the Department of Labor or another public agency.

Third, we should seek to establish a bona fide termination-of-employment safe harbor. Fourth, it would be very helpful to have model documentation for independent contracting and information that supports the special issues of independent contracting in the third age. Fifth, under current law, employers are allowed to set up a phased retirement program and under the program pay pension benefits from a defined-benefit plan to individuals who are still working after the age of 62. There is controversy about the appropriate age to enable such programs, and most employers that offer defined-benefit plans allow early retirement benefits at age 55. The age 62 requirement for these programs set forth in the Pension Protection Act (PPA) of 2006 should be reduced to a retirement plan's earliest allowed retirement age.

And last, several years ago regulations were proposed that would have clarified some of the unanswered questions about phased retirement. Those regulations were never completed, and regulations have still not been issued to clarify the phased retirement provisions of the PPA. The phased retirement regulations need to be finalized so that employers have assurance that programs will be in compliance.

The Future

At present, half of today's retirees are participating in some form of phased retirement, and more will choose this route in the future. It also appears that more companies will offer such a program in the future. In response to a question posed during a webcast sponsored by The Conference Board, 59 of 69 respondents stated that they planned to begin a phased retirement program within the next three years. This response reflects interest on the part of a significant number of companies, but it does not indicate whether most companies actually will offer programs because the respondents were people participating in a webcast on phased retirement. As I mentioned earlier, creating a better policy environment will go a long way toward improving the retirement options for both employee and employer. Ultimately, the goal is to have a strong phased retirement program in place that matches employer and employee needs and includes a portfolio of work options.

Conclusion

I am not advocating phased retirement solely because it enhances a retiree's overall financial security—although it may certainly play that role for many people—but, rather, because of its contribution to the overall retirement experience of retirees. A fulfilling, enjoyable retirement comes from having financial security and good health and also from engagement with the community. For many people, engagement is connected to work.

The official retirement age needs to and will rise, but it is important that retirees have the option to phase at whatever age they leave the labor force. Working longer (i.e., delaying retirement) is certainly important to financial security. But not everyone is in a position to work longer without making really difficult personal choices; for these people, phasing is an excellent option. The ability to choose phased retirement gives many people the opportunity to find the right work/life balance so that they can lead less stressful lives and can remain economically active. Society gains when employers can provide this flexibility to employees.

Question and Answer Session

Anna M. Rappaport

Question: Why are people working longer?

Rappaport: I think people work longer for financial and other reasons. A key reason is the need for more income. An added economic issue, particularly for workers younger than 65, is health insurance. Beyond the financial reasons, though, is the desire to engage and remain active. For many people, the workplace is a good environment in which to fulfill these needs.

Phased Retirement Is Not the Path to Retirement Security

Alicia H. Munnell
Director, Center for Retirement Research
Peter F. Drucker Professor of Management Sciences
Carroll School of Management, Boston College
Boston

As illustrated by the life-cycle savings model, the arithmetic of lower U.S. Social Security benefits and longer life expectancy adds up to people having to work longer, past the earliest retirement age of 62, and having to work full time to acquire the larger savings they will need during their retirement years. Because phased retirement is essentially part-time employment, it is not the solution to most retirees' primary challenge: building financial security. The energy spent on promoting phased retirement is a diversion from the real need of making it easier for older workers to work on a full-time basis until age 67.

How long people fully remain in the workforce is an important factor in their having enough money to live comfortably during retirement. Thus, phased retirement has only a limited ability to significantly enhance the average worker's path to financial security in retirement. I am certainly not opposed in principle to phased retirement; my concern is that proponents will spend all their energy fighting for phased retirement when what is really needed is for people to work longer in a full-time capacity.

At the most basic level, arithmetic will determine if phased retirement is a viable option for workers. At this juncture, I do not believe it is. U.S. Social Security benefits are already being reduced, and the Baby Boom Generation has been left holding a bag filled with severely depreciated 401(k)s. If people do not work longer in a full-time capacity, they simply will not have enough money in retirement. About 30 percent of the labor force retires earlier than they had planned—some by choice, some not. But the vast majority of retirement-age workers are able to exert some control over their employment situation as they age, and they need to. Taking the necessary steps, such as retraining, to maintain a competitive position in the workplace will be critical to older workers in order for them to save sufficient resources to support themselves during their retirement years.

Life-Cycle Savings Model

The life-cycle savings model shows that the amount of savings needed at retirement is based on the ratio of working years to retirement years. Workers who expect to have a lengthy retirement compared with their years spent on the job need a large amount of savings accumulated by retirement age. Conversely, if a short retirement period is anticipated, a much smaller pool of retirement savings will be needed. Because it is a fait accompli that the Social Security system will be providing less income to retirees, the life-cycle model indicates that people will have to work longer (or spend less) to make up the difference.

In 2002, the replacement rate—Social Security benefits as a percentage of preretirement earnings—for the average person was 41 percent. After including Medicare premiums, the rate drops to 39 percent. If we fast forward to 2030 and keep the retirement age at 65, the replacement rate falls to 36 percent. And bigger premiums will need to be taken out to cover Medicare B and D, thus reducing the replacement rate even further to 31 percent. Furthermore, the average Social Security recipient will be subject to income tax on the benefits, which lowers the rate even more to 29 percent. So, that is Social Security.

When anticipated retirement income drops, the life-cycle model suggests three possible responses: (1) save more while working, (2) adopt a lower standard of living in retirement, or (3) work longer. Baby Boomers who are quickly approaching retirement do not have enough time to make up the difference by saving more. Working longer is the key if they do not want to lower their standard of living in retirement. In 2008, workers who retired at age 62 received 75 percent of scheduled Social Security benefits; at age 66, 100 percent; and at age 70, 132 percent.

Viability of Phased Retirement

I do not believe that phased retirement is a viable option to help keep people in the workplace longer to build financial security before retiring. Most people indicate that they would like to phase in retirement, but I think this sentiment is similar to how one chooses to remove a Band-Aid—slowly peeling up the edges or just ripping it off. Many people would like to proceed slowly, to take off the Band-Aid gradually. According to the 2004 Health and Retirement Study (HRS) conducted by the University of Michigan, 55 percent of workers say that they would like to retire gradually, and based on 2005 AARP data, 38 percent are interested in participating in a phased retirement plan. The work environment is where most people have met their friends and have their daily social interactions, and it provides structure to their lives. Thus, people want to give it up only gradually. Phased retirement means more flexibility, and flexibility is generally good. The difficulty, however, is that it is not the road to retirement security, which is my singular concern. Nevertheless, enthusiasm for phased retirement has spread, even to the point that the U.S. Congress, with the Pension Protection Act of 2006, has made it possible for people to access their defined-benefit plans at age 62 instead of the normal retirement age for their company's plan.

But phased retirement may prove to be a disappointment. For example, data from the 2004 HRS indicate that phased retirement does not necessarily make people happier. A recent study compared the happiness of people who went into full retirement immediately with those who went gradually. The happiness of the participants was measured before they retired and then again after they had fully retired. The researchers found that the path to retirement—immediate or gradual—did not affect happiness. The critical variable was whether the retiree could exert control over *how* he or she chose to retire.

Most employers do not like phased retirement because it complicates matters regarding who is eligible for benefits. Another issue for employers is health insurance: Should workers who are phasing into retirement (phasing workers) continue to be covered by health insurance? If the employer provides health insurance to phasing retirees but not to younger, part-time workers, it creates a problem. And phased retirement involves part-time work, which, like all part-time work, presents scheduling and availability issues. It is also expensive because the employer has to allocate the hiring, monitoring, and reviewing functions—all necessary tasks of overseeing employees—over a smaller number of hours.

In 2007, two economists—Alan Gustman and Tom Steinmeier—tested retirement simulations when work hour restrictions were relaxed and found a big increase in part-time work.[1] About half of the increase in part-time workers came from people who would have otherwise completely retired, which actually increased the amount of work being done. But the other half of the increase in part-time workers came from people who would otherwise have worked full time, which actually decreased the amount of work being done. The net result appears to be that phasing has little effect on helping the employer get more work done.

The Answer: Work Longer

The average retirement age in the United States today is 63. That age needs to be moved up about four years to age 67 to compensate for the decline in Social Security replacement rates and the increase in Medicare premiums. The only practical answer is for people to work longer. A policy solution, such as phased retirement, would have little impact on the amount of work done. In order to make prolonged full-time work an effective solution for workers, employers will have to want to hire and retain older workers. The reality, however, is that no evidence exists that employers are particularly inclined to do so. In fact, studies on the productivity of older workers indicate that, at best, older workers are as productive as younger workers, but they could be less productive. And the problem with that finding is

---

[1] Alan L. Gustman and Thomas Steinmeier, "Projecting Behavioral Responses to the Next Generation of Retirement Policies," Working Paper 12958, National Bureau of Economic Research (March 2007).

that older workers are generally paid at least as much as younger workers but often more, especially when fringe benefits (in particular, defined-benefit plans for which costs rise as people age) are taken into account.

Figure 1 illustrates some of the findings from a study that I did with my colleagues Steven Sass and Mauricio Soto in 2006 on employer attitudes about older workers' productivity. We found that employers think older workers know the ropes and are good with customers, but they worry about older workers' ability to learn new tasks, their physical health and stamina, and their proximity to retirement. So, employers have mixed views of older workers.

Figure 1. Percentage of Employers Citing Positive or Negative Impact of Various Factors on Older Worker Productivity

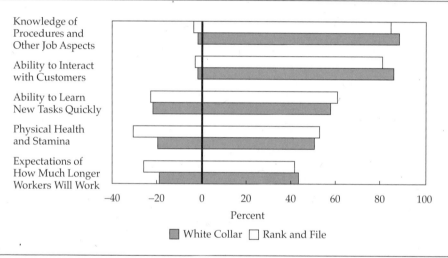

Source: Based on Alicia H. Munnell, Steven A. Sass, and Mauricio Soto, "Employer Attitudes towards Older Workers: Survey Results," Work Opportunity Briefs Series 3, Center for Retirement Research at Boston College (June 2006).

Thus, with skeptical employers, mobile older workers need to work full time to be attractive hires. Analysis of the Bureau of Labor Statistics' Current Population Survey data for male workers aged 58 to 62 in 1983 and 2006 shows that approximately the same percentage of workers (94 percent and 91 percent, respectively) worked full time in both years. But in 2006, fewer workers (46 percent compared with 70 percent in 1983) were working for the same employer that they had at age 50. Thus, the 46 percent of workers who changed employers since age 50 are mobile within the labor force. To find a job, these workers must make themselves as attractive as possible to employers, which generally translates into a demonstrated willingness to work on a full-time basis.

Of course, not everyone is able to work until age 67, nor is it fair to require that certain members of the older population work until age 67. For example, in 2000, the bottom quartile of males aged 50 had a disability-free life expectancy of 14 years; it is very difficult, as a society, to adopt a retirement policy that would require this population to work until age 67. I do not believe, however, that because a portion of the population cannot work until age 67, we should push for phased retirement for everybody. In 2006, 22 percent of men aged 50 to 64 had an activity limitation that could interfere with their ability to work. Based on life expectancy and physical limitation, approximately one-quarter of the older male population appears to face a challenge with working longer. My conclusion, therefore, is that it would be better to target our phased retirement efforts on those who stand to benefit most from such an approach rather than to try to achieve a phased retirement policy for all workers.

Conclusion

In the United States, we have a contracting retirement income system combined with an increasing life expectancy. Therefore, for retirees not to suffer a decline in their standard of living, they need to work longer. My view is that the phased retirement debate is a diversion from what we really need to focus on: helping older workers remain in full-time employment until at least age 67. The fact that employers often resist part-time employment provides more evidence that phased retirement is not the answer. Full-time employment is the answer, regardless of how stressful the job is or how stressful the work/life juggling act is.

Question and Answer Session

Alicia H. Munnell

Question: Why are people working longer?

Munnell: I work because I still enjoy it. A lot of people, however, need to work. Many probably don't have a 401(k) or a defined-benefit plan. They probably do have Social Security, but it isn't sufficient. The structure and social interaction in the workplace, too, are attractive to many older workers.

Question: How much is the cost of employer-provided health insurance coverage contributing to employers' lack of support of phased retirement?

Munnell: Providing health insurance benefits to older workers is a huge barrier to employers' support of phased retirement but also to part-time and full-time work. It makes all older employees a lot more expensive than younger employees. If we had national health insurance, this barrier would be removed, but we don't.

Question: How can we encourage people to delay claiming Social Security benefits, because doing so is usually in their best interest?

Munnell: The Social Security system itself is trying to educate people that it is in their best interest to delay filing for benefits. I have actually been collaborating with the Social Security Administration on a booklet about why retiring later is a good idea. Educating people about how valuable the income differential is for retiring later is very important.

For example, for those who retire at age 70, they receive 75 percent more income than if they had retired at age 62. Retiring later also has a very good effect on the survivor's benefit. Definitely a lot of education needs to be done, both by Social Security and by other organizations, to encourage people to retire later.

Question: Does the increasingly popular second career option have a role to play in easing the retirement burden on individuals and the Social Security system?

Munnell: Single-career employment is almost something of a historical notion at this point. The Urban Institute recently studied the nature of these new jobs, or second careers, held by older workers and found that, although they paid less and provided less in the way of fringe benefits, people generally liked these new jobs much better. They experienced less stress, and they were closer to their homes; the second career had a lot of positive attributes. So, yes, I do think that these second careers will play a role in allowing workers to continue working full time but in lower pressure jobs.

Question: What other considerations might be at play that are motivating workers to retire at age 62 rather than working longer?

Munnell: According to psychologists, as we age, we have a tendency to "positivize" or to divest ourselves of people and situations that we no longer enjoy. When I've asked retirees in the past "Why did you retire?" they gave what sounded like the most frivolous reasons: "I sat in the middle seat," "I was on the tarmac for two hours," "I'm just not doing this anymore," "I'm sick of it," or "I got a new, young boss, and I can't stand the guy, and I'm out of here."

The tendency to positivize also applies to the work environment. Our tolerance for putting up with things we don't like diminishes as we age. And then being able to receive Social Security benefits at age 62 really changes the calculation. It is important for people to understand what's influencing them and that they're more likely to call it quits on the spur of the moment as they grow older. Resisting that temptation is in their long-run best interest.

Effective Agency, Individual Involvement, and Default Choices

Richard Zeckhauser

Frank P. Ramsey Professor of Political Economy
Harvard University
Cambridge, Massachusetts

Defined-contribution plans put the investment burden on individuals. Given individuals' lack of expertise, many experts propose structuring investment defaults to nudge individuals' choices. Although this may be a necessary step, it is hardly sufficient. In the end, there is no substitute for intelligent discussion to establish the appropriate investment path customized to the needs of each individual.

We need effective "agency" (meaning experts faithfully helping those they are supposed to assist) for individuals making a critical but unusual decision, such as picking investments for their retirement nest egg. Effective agency, however, must be more than a mere matter of establishing a choice of defaults, or removing choices altogether. Consider retirees who are deciding how to structure their retirement income. Evidence shows that older people who are involved in making their own decisions do better in life. Given that quality of life should be our concern, and not just retirement security, we should want to get older people more involved in the financial decisions that affect them, not less.

The Importance of Individual Involvement and Preferences

Many of my colleagues focus excessively, often singularly, on default options. I think such a focus runs the risk of treating older people, indeed adults more generally, like children. My preference would be to place much more emphasis on treating the effective agency of critical decisions as requiring substantial input from the affected individual. Moreover, most important choices should be tailored to cater to people's individual preferences.

This latter point can be clarified with an example. I recently co-authored an article on prostate cancer. There are more than a half dozen primary treatments for prostate cancer, and a 70-year-old man (call him Rex) with prostate cancer will likely receive the default treatment. But what is the default treatment? It depends on which doctor Rex goes to. If Rex goes to Dr. Smith, he gets radiation. If Rex goes to Dr. Jones, he gets surgery. If Rex goes to Dr. Brown, he gets watchful waiting. The choice of treatment may depend modestly on Rex's condition, but mostly, it depends on Rex's doctor.[1]

The choice of treatment, however, should consider personal preferences and personality types. For example, with Dr. Brown as the patient's doctor, the "preferred" treatment for 70-year-old men with prostate cancer is watchful waiting. This option is a very good treatment for someone who can get up in the morning and go about his business without dwelling on the fact that he has prostate cancer, but I would maintain that this is not a good treatment for a man who would obsess every moment about his situation. And the trade-off between the risks of longevity and loss of sexual function surely depend on preferences as well.

Similarly, personal preferences and personalities should count for a great deal in terms of what individuals should do with respect to investment decisions and, particularly, lifetime consumption decisions. For instance, some of those who hold equities, particularly after the recent experience, will worry constantly about them, anticipating another late 2008 meltdown. Others, however, can hold equities without worrying about future crashes at all. People also have very different preferences for their lifetime consumption patterns.

Nevertheless, most financial planners are not good at asking clients such questions as, If things really went badly, would it be easy for you to live with your daughter? Could you reduce your consumption by 20 percent if needed? Would investment decisions that turned out poorly make you feel regret for the rest of your life?

My point is that people's preferences do differ, and decisions by advisers (agents) should be made in conjunction with the affected individuals and customized to their individual preferences and circumstances. The big challenge to our industry, I believe, is to find ways to create for many people the types of beneficial agency that many of us now provide for elderly relatives.

For example, most people have never had the opportunity to discuss with a financial planner how much their current savings rate would translate into in terms of retirement funds. If they did, more might realize that their current savings rate is woefully inadequate, thereby giving them the opportunity to make the necessary adjustments. We should give more people the chance to have this kind of discussion, rather than focus on designing and selecting default options.

Whose Default Options?

One point that I think we all can agree on is the need to save more. I would love to see the average American shift his or her savings rate up by 30 percent. But getting agreement on where those savings should be placed is quite another matter. Many

---

[1]Benjamin D. Sommers, Clair J. Beard, Anthony V. D'Amico, Irving Kaplan, Jerome P. Richie, and Richard Zeckhauser, "Predictors of Patient Preferences and Treatment Choices for Localized Prostate Cancer," *Cancer*, vol. 113, no. 8 (October 2008):2058–2067.

have argued that people should be more heavily invested in equities, which, of course, would not have worked out so well recently. Richard Thaler, who is one of the authors of the Save More Tomorrow[2] plan, observed in 1997: "for long-horizon investors, …we find the case for equities compelling" (p. 199).[3] But this position illustrates one problem with defaults. Although a heavy concentration in equities might be Thaler's preferred default for a young retiree, for someone like Zvi Bodie, who advocates a 100 percent annuity default, a heavy-equities option would be a terrible default. And of course, others would argue for yet different defaults. Moreover, a default option that works out badly, however desirable *ex ante*, subjects the agent to blame.

This hardly suggests that everyone should make investment decisions on his or her own without any guidance. For example, some of my noneconomist colleagues have been drawing what I think are inappropriate lessons from the dire current situation. They have concluded, based on their recent financial collapses, that they should spend more because their savings are likely to melt away. If I could talk with them for half an hour, I think I could convince them to pursue a more prudent course of action. So, clearly, I hardly recommend abandoning investors in general if even highly intelligent and well-educated people can easily get saving decisions disastrously wrong.

As is common, the middle course is best. The investment decision process should involve an expert agent providing some guidance but should give the affected individual significant involvement. A first step should be a discussion of preferences and tolerance for risk. This would also foster personalization of choices.

Conclusion

If nothing else, recent experience shows that many of the models developed to deal with financial situations should be called into question. Effective agency cannot be reduced to a set of default options. Rather, knowledgeable intelligence, with involvement by the individual, must be applied at every step along the way.

---

[2]Shlomo Benartzi and Richard H. Thaler, "Save More Tomorrow: Using Behavioral Economics to Increase Employee Saving," *Journal of Political Economy*, vol. 112, no. 1 (February 2004):S164–S187.
[3]Jeremy J. Siegel and Richard H. Thaler, "Anomalies: The Equity Premium Puzzle," *Journal of Economic Perspectives*, vol. 11, no. 1 (Winter 1997):191–200.

How Older People Behave

David Laibson
Harvard College Professor and
  Robert I. Goldman Professor of Economics
Harvard University
Cambridge, Massachusetts

Familiar issues trouble individuals nearing retirement and the pension systems intended to support them. But such less discussed topics as declining cognitive ability and unsound financial decision making are no less important to older adults.

In this presentation, I will talk about five familiar areas of concern before I turn to some less familiar issues.

Familiar Areas

In discussions of retirement savings, five areas are typically addressed: longevity, retirement timing, rapidly rising health care and long-term-care costs, slowing population growth, and the increasing need for households to make their own financial decisions.

First, longevity is increasing at the rate of about one month a year. Second, the timing of retirement has been relatively unresponsive to this increase in longevity. Although people are retiring a little later in the United States, people are retiring earlier in Europe. Third, health care and long-term-care costs are rapidly rising. One estimate is that health care costs, taken broadly, will rise from 15 percent of GDP to 29 percent of a larger GDP by 2040. Fourth, slowing population growth places additional strains on pay-as-you-go pension systems. And finally, governments and companies are transferring decision-making authority in many of these areas from institutions and fiduciaries to households.

This last point can be seen more clearly with some data on how the breakdown of private sector employees with a pure defined-benefit (DB) pension, a pure defined-contribution (DC) pension, or a DB and DC hybrid pension has changed over time, shown in **Figure 1**. In 1979, about 60 percent of households with a pension in the private sector had a pure DB pension. That number has now fallen to 10 percent. In contrast, pure DC pensions have risen from 17 percent to more than 60 percent in 2004.

Looked at in terms of the dollar breakdown of total retirement assets in the United States right now, as shown in **Exhibit 1**, of the total of $17.4 trillion of pension assets, about $4.4 trillion belongs to government employees, which is approximately

Figure 1. Pension Type as a Proportion of All Pensioned Private-Sector Workers, 1979–2004

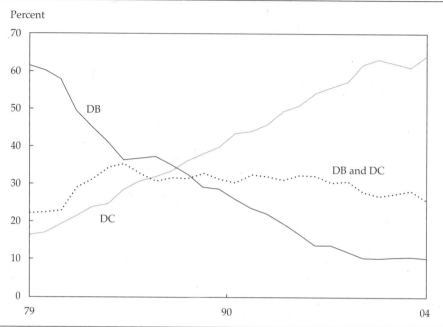

evenly divided between DB and DC funds. Of the other $13 trillion of private sector pension assets, only $2.4 trillion is in DB plans, with the remaining $10.6 trillion invested in other assets. Of this amount, $4.6 trillion is invested in IRAs, $4.4 trillion is invested in DC plans, and annuities constitute the remaining $1.6 trillion.

Exhibit 1. Breakdown of Retirement Assets in U.S. Market, Year-End 2007

Total U.S. retirement assets: $17.4 trillion		
Pension plans for government employees: $4.4 trillion	Private pension plans: $13.0 trillion	
	DB assets: $2.4 trillion	Other assets: $10.6 trillion
		IRA: $4.6 trillion
		DC: $4.4 trillion
		Annuities: $1.6 trillion

Source: Based on data from the Investment Company Institute.

Less Familiar Areas

In addition to these familiar concerns are some concerns that are perhaps less familiar but just as worrisome.

Cognitive Function. Cognitive function declines dramatically for older adults. On generic tests of analytical cognitive function ability, the average 20-year-old performs at about the 70th percentile among adults. But as people age, and not just for the very old but even the middle aged, performance robustly declines. By the later 80s, the average person in that age group is performing at about the 15th percentile on these cognitive function tests.[1]

Even more troubling is the growing incidence of fully diagnosed dementia. Dementia prevalence doubles every five years. For individuals in their early 60s, the prevalence of fully diagnosed dementia is about 1 percent. By the early 70s, prevalence grows to 3.3 percent. By the early 80s, it is around 13 percent, and by the late 80s, fully 30 percent of the adult population has fully diagnosed dementia.[2]

One might say that, at least from a financial perspective, this trend is not worrisome because once an individual has dementia, someone else will be managing his or her assets, which is largely true. That person, however, may not be trustworthy. The adviser may be charging outrageous fees or stealing in all sorts of different ways. But at least someone else is making the day-to-day decisions.

A related problem is that dementia does not come on all of a sudden. It comes first in the form of years and years of cognitive decline. At some point, individuals have significant cognitive impairment and are experiencing a great deal of trouble making all sorts of decisions but are nevertheless still very much in charge of their lives. For those in their 70s, approximately 16 percent of the population falls into this category, and for those in their 80s, it is about 30 percent.[3]

In particular, I want to point out the sum of two numbers. For those in their 80s, about 20 percent of the population has fully diagnosed dementia and about another 30 percent has cognitive impairment that is severe but not yet clinical dementia. We are talking about, in total, half of the population in their 80s not in a position to manage their own finances.

Bad Choices. When one examines the decisions made by older adults, these decisions look rather bad. In a paper by Agrawal, Driscoll, Gabaix, and myself, we looked at 10 different credit categories where we had comparative data across age

---

[1]Timothy Salthouse, "When Does Age-Related Cognitive Decline Begin?" *Neurobiology of Aging*, vol. 30, no. 4 (April 2009):507–514.

[2]C.P. Ferri, et al. "One Hundred Years On—The Global Prevalence of Dementia," *Lancet* (17 December 2005):2112–2117.

[3]Brenda L. Plassman, et al. "Prevalence of Cognitive Impairment without Dementia in the United States," *Annals of Internal Medicine*, vol. 148, no. 6 (18 March 2008):427–434.

groups.[4] We also had a rich array of controls: We knew these individuals' credit history; we knew their risk factors, their FICO scores; we knew their default histories. It is all in our database.

We then asked, What interest rate, controlling for all of those characteristics, did these individuals pay? It turns out that middle-aged adults are getting the best (i.e., lowest) interest rates, about 4.25 percent, shown in **Figure 2**. But because of lack of financial knowledge, lack of financial sophistication, and early symptoms of cognitive decline, older adults are doing relatively badly, much like younger adults who have their own deficits (deficits of experience). For those in their 80s, the interest rate on a home equity line rises to about 5 percent. Thus, they are paying more for their financial services.

In another study, my co-authors and I looked at a classic credit card gimmick.[5] A typical balance transfer offer goes something like this: If you transfer balances from one credit card to another, on the new card the transferred balances get a low interest rate, which sounds great, so you transfer $5,000. The gimmick is that if you use the new card to make a purchase and then you repay the card in light of that

Figure 2. Home Equity Credit Line Interest Rate (APR) by Borrower Age

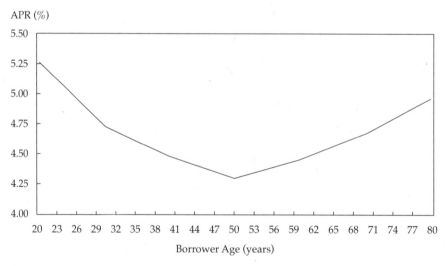

Note: APR = annual percentage rate.

---

[4]Sumit Agarwal, John C. Driscoll, Xavier Gabaix, and David I. Laibson, "The Age of Reason: Financial Decisions over the Lifecycle," NBER Working Paper No. 13191 (21 October 2008).
[5]Sumit Agarwal, John C. Driscoll, Xavier Gabaix, and David I. Laibson, "Learning in the Credit Card Market," NBER Working Paper No. 13822 (February 2008).

©2009 The Research Foundation of CFA Institute

purchase, your repayment does not go to the high interest rate balance that results from the new purchase. It goes instead to repay the balance that was transferred at the low rate. So, if you use the new card, you very rapidly end up repaying the balance that was transferred and now have a high interest rate on all the new debt. Basically, there was no gain for you.

How do you fix this problem? If you know enough, you have read the fine print so that you do not use the new card. You transfer balances and then you throw the new card into a drawer and do not touch it for eight months. That is certainly one way to exploit the offer.

Who reads the fine print, and who does not? It turns out that the people who never figure out this gimmick tend overwhelmingly to be the young and the old. The middle aged have a 30 percent chance of never figuring it out, and the old/young have about a 50 percent chance of never figuring it out. Again, we see the same pattern: The old are making more financial mistakes than their middle-aged cousins, although no more than the inexperienced young are making.

When it comes to retirement saving, it is not easy to compare retirement savings choices across the life cycle because, of course, different ages have different fundamental needs vis-à-vis savings. So, we looked at the old in isolation to determine how they are doing on an absolute basis, and we found that they are doing terribly. Adults older than age 59½ who have matches in a 401(k) have a perfect arbitrage because they can contribute, get the free match, and then take the money out of the plan if they needed it without any penalty because they are already older than age 59½. But it turns out that only half of older adults take advantage of this opportunity by at least contributing up to the match threshold.[6] In other words, half are failing this fundamental financial IQ test with enormous consequences for their personal balance sheet. They are giving away about 1.6 percent of their income each year simply by failing to take this free money. In addition, we found that educating these people by using a simple four-page educational intervention did not work. Perhaps other education might work, but our educational intervention showed no effect.

Conclusion

We need to put less emphasis on providing a wide variety of investment choices and more emphasis on helping people make the right decisions; automaticity is the theme here. We need to automate the accumulation phase and automate the decumulation phase, perhaps allowing opt-outs but certainly encouraging people to stay with these defaults.

---

[6]James Choi, David Laibson, and Brigitte C. Madrian, "Plan Design and 401(k) Savings Outcomes," *National Tax Journal*, vol. 57, no. 2 (2004):275–298.

We also need fiduciary oversight for retirees. At the moment, we provide adequate regulation inside the 401(k) envelope. But once you retire, you are on your own. No one is looking over your shoulder other than maybe your broker, who often has every interest in misguiding you.

Finally, we have to think seriously for the first time about how to create trust structures that are inexpensive and scalable. A generation is about to retire with enormous wealth that they directly control, and they will need to delegate decision making to a third party before their ability to make decisions declines.

Dutch Stand-Alone Collective Pension Schemes: The Best of Both Worlds?

Lans Bovenberg
Scientific Director
Netspar, Tilburg University
Tilburg, the Netherlands

European pension systems are in crisis. Governments and employers are withdrawing as plan sponsors, making institutional innovation imperative. Collective, stand-alone pension plans—as seen in the Dutch system—offer an attractive hybrid model between corporate defined-benefit plans and individual defined-contribution plans.

The pension system in Europe is in crisis. Hence, institutional innovation is needed. The purpose of this presentation, therefore, is to describe the nature of the pension crisis and the various ways of dealing with it, placing particular emphasis on the evolving Dutch system.

Troubles in the Pension System

Europe's pension system is built on three pillars: (1) public pay-as-you-go pension plans, (2) corporate defined-benefit plans, and (3) individual defined-contribution plans.

Public pension plans are the dominant form in most European countries. In Germany, France, and Spain, for example, such plans account for all but a small percentage of current pension income. In the Netherlands, Switzerland, and to some extent the United Kingdom, corporate defined-benefit plans help share the burden by making up a significant proportion of pension income, as shown in **Table 1**. But now, both governments and corporations are withdrawing from the pension business, so an increasing number of citizens have to rely on the third pillar of individual defined-contribution plans. This places a complex responsibility on individuals—one that they are, in many cases, not well prepared for.

Public Pay-as-You-Go Plans. The core of the problem with pay-as-you-go plans is that the large countries of continental Europe are heavily dependent on them despite the fact that they must supplement such plans with additional funded components—especially for people in the middle and higher income brackets. As birth rates drop substantially below replacement levels in such countries, the human capital needed to fund pay-as-you-go systems inevitably declines. After all, with fewer working young adults paying for larger numbers of older adults, pay-as-you-go systems become unsustainable. European policymakers realize, therefore,

Table 1. Percentage of Pension Income by Type of Plan

Plan Type	Netherlands	Germany	France	Italy	Spain	Switzerland	United Kingdom	United States
First pillar: Pay-as-you-go plans	50%	85%	79%	74%	92%	42%	65%	45%
Second pillar: Corporate defined-benefit plans	40	5	6	1	4	32	25	13
Third pillar: Individual defined-contribution plans	10	10	15	25	4	26	10	42

Source: Based on data from Axel Börsch-Supan, "International Comparison of Household Savings Behaviour: The German Savings Puzzle," MEA Discussion Paper 02006, Mannheim Research Institute for the Economics of Aging, University of Mannheim (January 2002).

that as human capital declines as a result of low fertility, more investment must be made in physical and financial capital. By expanding the sources of pension funding, countries gain not only additional capital but also opportunities for better diversification of political, demographic, and financial risk. Many Europeans, however, are understandably having second thoughts about alternative forms of funding because they worry that funded pensions are likely to be expensive and risky. In fact, they have seen evidence for such concern in the two other prevalent forms of pension finance: funded defined-benefit and defined-contribution plans.

Corporate Defined-Benefit Plans. Just as governments are looking for alternatives to pay-as-you-go systems, corporations are looking for alternatives to defined-benefit plans, which are becoming increasingly expensive. To illustrate, pension obligations already have risen substantially compared with wage income in the Netherlands as a result of aging and maturing of the pension system. If no changes to the system are made, the stock of pension obligations is likely to increase to more than four times wage income by 2030. Given these developments, many companies will find their core businesses dwarfed by their responsibilities as *de facto* insurers. Furthermore, because new accounting rules for pension plans require more transparency, employers and policymakers are beginning to realize that defined-benefit plans, which were clearly mispriced in the past (because actuaries understated the cost by using too high a discount rate), are far more expensive than they had thought, especially in an environment where interest rates are low.

Employers and policymakers are not the only ones who are concerned. Workers, too, are waking up to the fact that these systems are quite risky for them because workers actually bear the credit risk of the corporations that have promised them pension benefits. Europe does not have the same extensive quasi-public insurance systems for corporate defined-benefit plans that exist in the United States,[1] so workers are beginning to realize that they should diversify their assets better in the capital market. Finally, because of the implicit options that are being written by the different parties to defined-benefit plans, many possibilities for conflicts of interest exist among the various stakeholders. For example, companies provide implicit put options to workers by agreeing to make up funding shortages. At the same time, however, the bankruptcy risk of companies implies that workers, as creditors of the company, provide an implicit put option to the shareholders of the company.[2] For these and other reasons, the defined-benefit system is declining in popularity.

Individual Defined-Contribution Plans. Defined-contribution plans also have their share of problems. Three flaws come immediately to mind. First, many individuals simply do not have the background or interest to make complex investment decisions. Second, because many individuals delegate their investment decisions for this reason, problems of governance arise. Among these are principal–agent conflicts, lack of bargaining power on the part of the worker/investor, and inadequate product design (e.g., excessive choice, high expenses, and imperfect risk management). Third, the market for retirement investment vehicles is imperfect. Annuity markets suffer from selection risk, counterparty risk, and exorbitant pricing, and the financial instruments needed to protect against macro risks—such as longevity, standard-of-living, and inflation risk—are not widely available.

Responses to Pension System Problems

Because of the flaws in the first two pillars of European pension systems, governments and corporations are removing this risk from their balance sheets by withdrawing as plan sponsors. They are placing the responsibility for retirement security in the hands of the affected individuals, who are now expected to fund the third pillar of the European pension system. But individuals are as imperfect as the financial markets they are supposed to be navigating in. My argument, therefore, is that collective, stand-alone pensions offer an attractive middle way between corporate defined-benefit plans and individual defined-contribution plans.

Collective, Stand-Alone Pension Plans. A collective, stand-alone pension plan is a funded plan established by a group of people who wish to pool their mortality risk so can they obtain annuity payments (that is, a pension) at a fair

---

[1]The Pension Benefit Guaranty Corporation (PBGC) in the United States is referred to as quasi-public because, although organized by the government, it is funded entirely with insurance premiums collected from the corporate participants.

[2]The options are not offsetting because the first put option has value only if the company survives and the second has value only if the company goes bankrupt.

price and with minimal risk. In U.S.-centric terms, it is a mutual (participant-owned and nonprofit) life insurance company with one product, a life annuity.[3] The annuity may be fixed or variable.

To minimize adverse selection risk, such plans must be compulsory (or at least be the default choice) for a relatively large group of people. (The compulsory or default aspect also mitigates imperfect individual decision making and saves on transaction costs.) The pools are typically based on the industry people work in but can also be based on the profession of the participants. A pool may also be a voluntary association, but this practice increases the risk of adverse selection and adds marketing costs. I refer to such plans as "stand-alone" plans because the risks are not guaranteed by corporate sponsors but by the invested contributions of the employees themselves. The plans can trade the risks on capital markets or contract with insurance companies to cover the risks. Such funds have the advantage of being explicitly owned by the participants, so they serve the interests only of the participants, not those of a corporation or a governmental unit. Finally, collective plans allow for division of labor and economies of scale. For example, the collectives can contract their administration to for-profit organizations.

The Dutch Pension System. The Dutch system provides an example of how a collective, stand-alone plan can be coordinated with other parts of a national pension system. As I mentioned earlier, the first pillar in the Netherlands is the government-provided pension—a flat amount that everyone receives. Its explicit purpose is to keep people out of poverty and is based on the minimum wage. Because of this pension program, old-age poverty in the Netherlands is quite low. Even so, the system leaves plenty of room for individual responsibility; people who want more than a minimum income in retirement must look to the private sector.

Fortunately, the private sector in the Netherlands has taken up this responsibility. Indeed, the Dutch corporatist tradition encourages employer organizations and unions to cooperate through collective bargaining and sectoral agreements. Such agreements act as the second pillar of the Dutch pension system and are encouraged by the government in two ways. First, the government provides tax benefits to those who participate. Second, when the unions and the employer organizations come to an agreement, the government makes these agreements semi-compulsory for all companies in a particular industry. Thus, more than 90 percent of the employees are covered.

These nongovernmental programs are run as defined-benefit plans because they are earnings related and the benefits are paid as annuities; thus, they are explicitly retirement products. This employment-related tier of the Dutch system has changed over the past 10 years, evolving from pure defined-benefit plans to

---

[3]The annuity can be single life or, in the case of a married couple, second to die.

hybrid plans in which only part of the nominal pension right is guaranteed and the rest (i.e., the indexation to wages or prices) is an aspirational target. In effect, the second pillar thus features a defined-benefit component *and* a defined-contribution component. It includes back loading of benefits and is built on a cooperative arrangement with a governing board appointed by social partners, with benefits linked to employment history.

Under such programs, risks are increasingly being borne by the people who have the pension rights, rather than those who are the contributors. Because of an aging workforce, pension obligations are rising faster than the premium base. Therefore, contributions have become much less effective as a risk-sharing device. If assets fall in value and the premium base is relatively small, contributions must be increased significantly to compensate for a relatively small decline in assets. It is inevitable, therefore, that the pensioners—the people who hold the pension rights—be asked to take on more risk.

Furthermore, these programs have moved from a final pay system to a career average system. Under the final pay system, the pension benefit is determined by the retiree's final income and is thus automatically linked to wage developments during the working life. But with a career average system, the pension rights of the active members (i.e., the members who are still in the workforce and still paying premiums) must be indexed to wages to prevent pension rights from being eroded in real terms. This indexation, however, is conditional on the financial health of the fund. Hence, the indexation mechanism has become more powerful in absorbing risks.

Strengths of the Dutch System. Nongovernmental (or occupational) plans, the second pillar of the Dutch system, have five distinct strengths. First, the funds are stand alone, which helps avoid risk because the people who hold the pension rights are not exposed to the credit risk of a corporate sponsor. Moreover, ownership of the assets rests solely with the members. There is no concern that the shareholders of the participating companies might have a claim on any pension fund surplus.

Second, complex investment decisions are delegated to highly trusted cooperatives that are run in the interest of the members. These cooperatives are nonprofits with strong involvement by unions and employer organizations. Third, the cooperatives contract administration to for-profit professionals, which not only brings in expertise but also helps lower expenses by establishing competition at the wholesale level. Fourth, the Dutch system uses advanced risk management aimed at retirement security. Indeed, interest rate risks are managed by integrating the accumulation phase with the payout phase.

These plans thus complete the retirement services provided by the financial markets. In fact, the plans are designed to trade between participants those risks—such as standard of living risk and longevity risk—that are not yet traded in the market. By pooling longevity risks among a large group of people, the plans mitigate selection risk.

Improvements Needed for the Dutch System. In spite of these strengths, further improvements are called for.

First, the system needs more complete risk-sharing contracts. Because the population is aging, pension obligations (as discussed earlier) are rising faster than premiums, thus increasing the risk in the system. Therefore, it becomes more important to be explicit about risk sharing. **Figure 1** offers another way to look at the current way that risk is shared. The horizontal axis represents the assets of a pension fund. The assets needed to fund a given nominal obligation are represented by L^N, and the assets needed to fund a real (inflating) obligation having the same initial benefit as the nominal obligation—the ambition of the fund—are represented by L^R. For asset levels between L^N and L^R, the contract is complete in the sense that the fund balance determines how much indexation the fund can afford. But the contract does not prescribe what happens when the fund has more assets than L^R or fewer assets than L^N. What to do in such cases is left to the discretion of the governing board of the pension fund. It would be better to make the contract more complete; if everyone agrees on exactly how to share risk *ex ante*, the likelihood of a disagreement *ex post* is decreased. Unfortunately, a lot of companies are getting close to L^N, which means we will have a chance to see what happens.

Figure 1.   Inflation Risk Sharing for a Typical Dutch Pension Plan

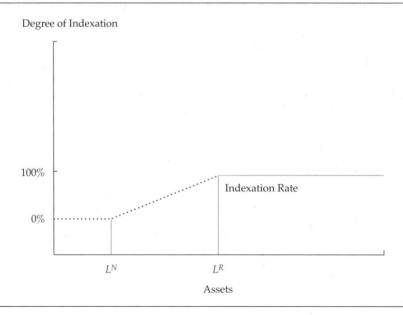

Second, more advanced risk sharing is needed between generations. The current system is offering the wrong guarantees to the wrong people. All guarantees are now in nominal terms, and it would be better to have them in real terms. Furthermore, the system guarantees pension benefits to everyone, regardless of age. But we could make the system more efficient by being more selective about who receives guarantees and who benefits more from the equity premium.

Third, if we assign more risk to participants, we ought to give them more flexibility in absorbing such risk. Such risk can be absorbed in two possible ways. One is the consumption–savings margin; if the economy experiences a downturn, the default contribution can be increased to help make up for what people have lost. The labor–leisure margin would also be important, but in the Netherlands, we still have compulsory retirement, which currently makes it difficult to ask people to work longer to make up for investment losses. Therefore, the Netherlands needs to make the labor market for the elderly more flexible so that we can use the labor–leisure margin to absorb risk. In addition, we need to consider dealing with various risks in different ways. For example, longevity risk should not necessarily be dealt with in the same manner as investment risk; longevity risk can be greatly reduced through pooling, whereas investment risk cannot.

Fourth, the retirement age should be adjusted for expected changes in longevity. Fifth, benefits are highly back-end loaded: The price a person is charged for a deferred annuity does not depend on the person's age. Everyone pays the same annuity premium. Of course, this means that, actuarially, the young pay too much and the old, too little. This practice creates a lot of cross-subsidies in the system. This was not a problem when most people stayed in the same sector throughout their lives, but it is now becoming a problem that causes all kinds of distortions.

Sixth, governance issues must be handled more professionally and in the interests of those bearing the risk. New rules that decrease the level of discretion now given unions and employer groups should be established. Furthermore, because participants (both retirees and active workers who have built up pension rights in the fund), rather than the people who contribute the premiums, are increasingly taking on the role of risk bearers, the consequences of this change for governance must be considered.

Conclusion

European pension systems are in crisis. Government and employer sponsors are withdrawing, making institutional innovation imperative. Collective, stand-alone pension plans offer an attractive hybrid between corporate defined-benefit plans and individual defined-contribution plans. The Dutch system, which is moving toward stand-alone pension funds, offers a useful model to consider. It has many strengths but needs further innovations to assure its success in the long term.

When I consider applying such a system to other countries, several possibilities come to mind. Employers and governments can act as plan sponsors (in the sense of organizers) but can be relieved of the onus of being risk bearers. For small employers, multiemployer plans can be devised. Whereas I would recommend compulsory participation in most continental European countries, I believe that default participation would work best in the United Kingdom and the United States. Finally, to help guide individuals in making the right decisions about their retirement funding, specialized professional institutions should be established. For governance purposes, I prefer nonprofit cooperatives that combine the best attributes of collective decision making and competition.